T0319956

Public Microeconomics

To Maureen

Public Microeconomics

Efficiency and Equity in Public Policy

Joaquim Silvestre

University of California, Davis, USA

Edward Elgar
Cheltenham, UK • Northampton, MA, USA

Published by
Edward Elgar Publishing Limited
The Lypiatts
15 Lansdown Road
Cheltenham
Glos GL50 2JA
UK

Edward Elgar Publishing, Inc.
William Pratt House
9 Dewey Court
Northampton
Massachusetts 01060
USA

A catalogue record for this book
is available from the British Library

Library of Congress Control Number: 2012930583

MIX
Paper from
responsible sources
FSC® C018575

ISBN 978 0 85793 207 5

Typeset by Servis Filmsetting Ltd, Stockport, Cheshire
Printed and bound by MPG Books Group, UK

Contents

· ·

Preface and acknowledgments

• •

The present book is based on my Public Microeconomics lectures at the University of California, Davis. The course is structured as the first half, centered in externalities and public goods, of a two-quarter sequence. The second half, not covered here, concerns taxation.

The book is unapologetically theoretical. It emphasizes the essential ideas, and the connections among them. It strives for clarity and precision, integrating three forms of discourse: (i) verbal, (ii) graphical and (iii) algebraic and calculus-based. Elementary calculus is used frequently. Upper division economics students have had, in most schools, at least one quarter of calculus: they may as well use it. We do the students no service if we retreat to a calculus-free upper division, as most textbooks on the topic seem to favor. On the contrary, making them comfortable with the mathematical tools that they learned in the prerequisite calculus courses develops their ability to think clearly, communicate precisely and argue conclusively on economic issues.

The book presents established theory in sometimes novel ways, and offers the conceptual instruments for applying social welfare criteria to environmental economics, political economy, the pricing of public goods and public utilities, and social insurance. The discussion is organized around the First Fundamental Theorem of Welfare Economics, and strives to maintain the dual normative perspective of efficiency and equity. Instrumentally, it often employs user-friendly utility functions which are (strictly) concave transformation of a quasilinear function.[1] This makes the formal analysis simple and operational, conducive to computationally easy examples and exercises. On the other hand, concavity implies that all marginal utilities are decreasing and that the utility possibilities frontiers are concave, permitting the analysis of equity and fairness issues together with efficiency.

The choice of topics and style is deeply, if distantly, influenced by my graduate studies at the University of Minnesota under the guidance of John S. Chipman, Leo Hurwicz and Hugo Sonnenschein. Throughout the years I have learned enormously from Andreu Mas-Colell and from

---

[1] I employed this innovation in J. Silvestre (2003) "Wicksell, Lindahl and the theory of public goods," *Scandinavian Journal of Economics*, 105(4), 527–553.

John E. Roemer: this book owes much to them, and I am deeply indebted to both.[2]

Communication is undemanding in this age of the internet: readers and users of the book are encouraged to send their feedback by emailing jbsilvestre@ucdavis.edu. It will be genuinely appreciated. Exercises are available on request.

Davis, California, September 2011

[2] In particular, our collaborations on public microeconomics have trickled down, in a diffuse way, to parts of this book, e.g., A. Mas-Colell and J. Silvestre (1989), "Cost share equilibria: A Lindahlian approach," *Journal of Economic Theory*, 47(2), 239–256; J.E. Roemer and J. Silvestre (1992), "A welfare comparison of public and private monopoly," *Journal of Public Economics*, 48, 67–81; J.E. Roemer and J. Silvestre (1993), "The proportional solution in economies with both private and public ownership," *Journal of Economic Theory*, 59(2), 426–444, and Humberto Llavador, J.E. Roemer and J. Silvestre (2011), "A dynamic analysis of human welfare in a warming planet," *Journal of Public Economics*, 95 (11–12), 1607–1620.

Foreword to students

The economics of the book is reasonably self-contained, but some of the material is directly related to that of a standard course in intermediate microeconomics, with which it shares methods and mode of analysis.

Intermediate microeconomics considers mostly the interaction among private economic agents (such as consumers and firms) through markets, particularly competitive markets. Public microeconomics is centered in the economic activity of the government, resulting from the interaction through the political system and from cooperation. This activity is often motivated by the need to alleviate some ill effects of noncooperative interaction, for instance, among externality-generating agents. But in actuality more often than not public policy is oriented towards achieving ethical and distributional objectives. Policy recommendations should be governed by the dual social normative criteria of efficiency and equity. This book emphasizes both.

The present text aspires at granting similar weights to three forms of reasoning and exposition, namely: (i) verbal, (ii) graphical and (iii) mathematical. The calculus material is elementary, but extensively employed.[1] It may be useful to review graphs, algebra, equations, the concept of a derivative, the chain rule and the fundamental theorem of calculus. The derivative, $a - bx$, of the function $ax - 0.5bx^2$ will appear every other page, so to speak. Perhaps when you studied calculus you were wondering what was the usefulness of it all. It is hoped that the book will provide some answers.

To the extent that it is possible, the book attempts to be at the same time concept-intensive, graph-intensive and math-intensive. The objective is to develop, via practice, the ability to move effortlessly among words, graphs and mathematical expressions. Some people (not everybody) feel more comfortable with words than with graphs or math: after all, we learn to speak earlier. But using language with clarity and precision is harder than it looks. The effort to express ideas and arguments graphically and formally often pays in terms of the accuracy, elegance and persuasiveness of the language employed.

---

[1] The footnotes and the appendices may contain slightly more abstract math: they are essentially optional, and may be skipped on a first reading (except this one). The notation for functions consistently uses round parentheses: $f(x - y)$ is read "the value of the function f at point $(x - y)$, whereas $q[x - y]$ means the product of the numbers q and $x - y$".

1 Introduction

1.1 Positive vs. normative analysis

Two modes of analysis are employed in economics, namely *positive* and *normative*. Positive analysis aims at understanding "how things are," i.e., at explaining how the economy works, and at forecasting the reaction of the economic system to changes in the environment or in policy. A positive question is about *facts*.

Normative analysis, on the contrary, focuses on "what should be done." It seeks to evaluate alternatives and to justify policy recommendations. Of course, it presupposes an understanding of the positive issues, but it also necessitates social decision criteria. These are founded on the basic principles of *efficiency*, on the one hand, and of *distributive justice*, *equity* or *fairness*, on the other. A normative question is about *social desirability*.

Efficiency criteria aim at assessing "the size of the social pie." The central notion is that of *economic efficiency*, based on the *Pareto criterion*: see Sections 1.4 and 1.6 below. A derived criterion, namely that of *potential compensation*, underpins many surplus-type measures such as those provided by cost–benefit analysis (see Appendix 1D below).

The criteria of distributive justice evaluate the social desirability of the way "the pie is shared:" see Section 1.5 below. *Welfarist* criteria, traditional in economics, focus on the final distribution of welfare. More recently, the emphasis has been placed on equalizing opportunities ("leveling the playing field"), an approach that stresses personal responsibility.[1]

1.2 Social interaction and equilibrium

Positive economics views economic activity as the result of the *interaction* among decision makers, agents or actors, such as consumers and firms. The interaction may take place in various forms and through various institutions.

---

[1] See J.E. Roemer (1996), *Theories of Distributive Justice*, and J.E. Roemer (1998), *Equality of Opportunity*, both published by Harvard University Press, Cambridge, MA.

1. Atomistic, or perfectly competitive, markets;
2. Markets where some agents have market power, such as oligopolistic markets;
3. Physical interaction, as in environmental externalities;
4. Cooperation, as within a firm or among users of a collective irrigation system;
5. The political system.

We assume that the interacting agents have well-defined preferences, which they optimize subject to the relevant constraints. The constraints may be physical, institutional or determined by the economic conditions that they face.

Interaction form (1) is modeled by the *competitive market equilibrium* model, which can also be called the *supply and demand* model, or, in their more sophisticated versions, the *general competitive equilibrium*, *Walrasian*, or *Arrow–Debreu* model.[2] The decision makers are consumers and firms, who trade in a number of goods. The model views each agent as if she were trading with an impersonal market, where the prices of the various goods are posted. Given those prices, each agent decides how much of each good to buy or sell. A *competitive (market) equilibrium* obtains when these planned purchases and sales match in the aggregate.

Under some conditions, a competitive market equilibrium is efficient: see the *First Fundamental Theorem of Welfare Economics* in Chapter 2 below. But if one of these conditions is not satisfied, then the competitive equilibrium is typically not efficient: we then say that a *market failure* occurs.

Interaction forms (2) and (3) are often modeled as (noncooperative) *games*, a more general paradigm of social interaction. In a game, every agent interacts with any other agent, and the welfare of an agent depends on her (meaning her or his) actions as well as on everybody else's actions. A *Cournot–Nash equilibrium* obtains when each agent is doing what is best for her given what the others are doing: see Appendix 1B below for details.[3] It turns out that, more often than not, Cournot–Nash equilibria are inefficient, the First Fundamental Theorem of Welfare Economics

---

[2] Named after Léon Walras (1834–1910), Kenneth Arrow (born 1921) and Gérard Debreu (1921–2004). Arrow was awarded the Nobel Prize in Economic Sciences in 1972, and Debreu in 1983.

[3] Named after Augustin Cournot (1801–1877) and John Nash (born 1928). Nash was awarded the Nobel Prize in Economic Science in 1994. John von Neumann and Oskar Morgenstern contributed to the development of the analysis in their *Theory of Games and Economic Behavior* (1944), Princeton: Princeton University Press.

notwithstanding: the perfectly competitive equilibrium model portrays an idealized, limited case of social interaction.

Whether efficient or not, neither competitive equilibria nor Cournot–Nash equilibria can be presumed to satisfy any criterion of distributive justice. Societies address distributive justice concerns by interaction forms (4) and (5) above, namely cooperation and public policy.

1.3   Government and markets

One may naïvely believe that interaction forms (1) and (5) are in conflict, more government meaning less market development. In reality, however, they are complementary. The last few centuries have experienced substantial expansions of both governments and markets. And cross-country studies have shown a positive correlation between the share of government in the economy and the weight of markets. Figure 1.1 reproduces Figure 1 in Timothy Besley and Torsten Persson (2009):[4] it shows a positive correlation between a measure of government capacity, namely the share of income taxes in GDP, and a measure of financial development, namely the ratio of private credit to GDP.

The operation of markets and of the government has both *allocative* effects (i.e., on the allocation of resources and the production and consumption of the various goods and services), which are normatively evaluated by *efficiency* criteria, and *distributive* effects (i.e., on the income, wealth and welfare levels of individuals and families), normatively evaluated by criteria of *distributive justice*.

Many government activities have primarily allocative aims. Examples are:

1. The *provision of public goods by direct supply*, such as the legal and judicial system, monetary, financial and trade frameworks, defense, infrastructure and various forms of information.
2. The provision of some goods that are essentially *private goods*, such as social insurance, health, education. These policies are often motivated both by market failures and by distributive justice concerns.
3. The *intervention in markets*, again often aimed at counteracting market failures, such as the regulation of financial markets and public utilities, the taxation of activities that generate negative externalities (pollution) and the subsidization of positive externality-causing activities (such as education).

---

[4] "The origins of state capacity: Property rights, taxation and politics," *American Economic Review*, 99(4), 1218–1244.

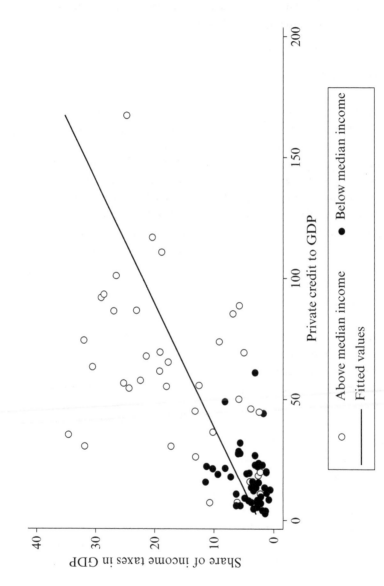

Figure 1.1 *Correlation between share of income taxes in GDP and ratio of private credit to GDP in various countries, 1995 data (Figure 1 in Besley and Persson, 2009)*

These activities may indirectly wield important distributional consequences even when they are not directly targeted to distribution (consider,
for instance, free-trade agreements, or military expenditures). In addition,
these policies must be financed by taxes or user fees, or by the issuance of
debt, which do have clear distributional implications.

Conversely, policies with distributive primary objectives, such as progressive taxation, antipoverty programs or price supports for agricultural
products, often have allocative effects via incentives.

1.4 Efficiency

1.4.1 The Pareto criterion

The Pareto criterion is based on the unanimous agreement of all members
of society.[5]

Definition. Feasible alternative *A Pareto-dominates* alternative *B* if nobody
prefers *B* to *A* and at least one person prefers *A* to *B*.

The notion presupposes that the set of feasible alternatives is well defined:
see Section 1.6 below.

Perhaps the Pareto criterion is not terribly practical, because it seldom
happens that everybody agrees.[6] But it is rather incontrovertible: society
should not have preferences contradicting the unanimous sentiment of all
its members. It would otherwise fall into dictatorship or paternalism.

The Pareto criterion does present some subtleties. It implicitly
assumes that society is comprised of a given set of individuals, with clear
and unarguable preferences. But in actuality some issues may arise.

1. Do we include infants and children in the list of members of society?
   A possible standpoint is that children's preferences are by definition
   included in those of their parents, and hence they should not be separ-
   ately considered. But many present-day norms (compulsory education, the prohibition of child labor and child abuse) view the interests
   of children as separate from those of their parents.
2. Do we include future generations? One position is that, if they are
   not here, they do not directly count: perhaps they indirectly count to
   the extent that parents care about the welfare of their children, which

---

[5] Named after Vilfredo Pareto (1848–1923).

[6] This difficulty has led to the *potential compensation criterion*, see Appendix 1D
below.

in turn includes that of the grandchildren of the present generation, and so on. But many of the current policy discussions on government debt, social security, quality of the environment and global warming assume that present society has duties relative to future generations beyond the preferences of the current generation.

3. Possible distinctions among *preferences*, *needs*, *tastes*, *interests* and *whims* are not terribly useful for positive economics, but are crucial in normative economics. In particular, preferences based on erroneous information have lower normative value than well-informed preferences.

4. Many of us have preferences on the welfare or consumption of other people. Should these preferences count? For instance, Ms. Virginia may prefer that young people abstain from extramarital sex. Mr. Just may prefer living in a society where abject poverty has been eradicated. Mr. Green, who earns $3,000 a month, may prefer that everybody's income be capped at $100,000. Should any of these preferences count for the definition of social welfare?

1.4.2   Pareto efficiency

Definition. Feasible alternative A is *Pareto efficient* if no feasible alternative Pareto-dominates A.

Again, the notion presupposes that the set of feasible alternatives is well defined.

The definition is both simple and thorny, because it is defined by a negative sentence: if *no* (feasible) alternative Pareto-dominates A, then A *is* Pareto efficient. If, on the contrary, *there exists* a feasible alternative that Pareto dominates A, then A *is not* Pareto efficient.

Observe that Pareto efficiency is a Yes–No proposition, not a matter of degree. We cannot say "more Pareto efficient" or "very Pareto efficient."

As noted, because the Pareto criterion is based on the idea of unanimous agreement, it may have a limited practical scope. Given two alternatives, it may well occur that neither one Pareto dominates the other one: this will necessarily be the case if both alternatives are efficient, and may occur even if one of them is efficient and the other is not.

1.4.3   The Pareto criterion and the utility possibilities set

There are many people in a real-life society, but the main ideas can be expressed in a hypothetical society with only two people, named Ms. Blue and Mr. Red. Everything that refers to Blue (resp. Red) will be subscripted by B (resp. R). We postulate a quantitative index of the level of personal welfare, standard of living or *utility*, which in particular represents the person's preferences: a person prefers alternatives with higher utility. Denote U_B and U_R the utility levels reached by Blue and Red, respectively. Some utility pairs (U_B, U_R) will be feasible given the conditions in this economy, i.e., will be reached at feasible situations or alternatives of the economy, while some other imaginable utility pairs will not be feasible. The set of all feasible (U_B, U_R) pairs is called the *utility possibilities set* of the economy, and its northeastern boundary the *utility possibilities frontier*.

The set and the frontier may look like those in Figure 1.2. Observe first that point A lies northeast of B, which means that at point A the utility of both people is higher than at B: both people are better off at the alternative of the economy that yields the utility pair of A than at that of B. Hence, the alternative that yields A Pareto-dominates the alternative that yields B. Similarly, the alternative that corresponds to point C Pareto-dominates that of point B. Second, point A corresponds to a Pareto efficient alternative of the economy (there is no attainable utility pair northeast of A), whereas B and C correspond to inefficient alternatives. Third, neither the alternative of utility pair A (which is Pareto efficient) Pareto-dominates that of C (because Ms. Blue has higher utility at C), nor the alternative of C Pareto dominates that of A (because Mr. Red has higher utility at C). These two alternatives are Pareto noncomparable. Last, the alternative of point D is Pareto efficient, even though utilities are markedly unequal there.

1.5 Distributive justice

1.5.1 Social welfare functions

As just seen, Pareto efficiency is consistent with a high degree of inequality. A state where Mr. Red has everything and Ms. Blue has nothing may be efficient. Extreme inequality is socially undesirable, even if economic efficiency is achieved.

At the end of the 19th century, economists and philosophers proposed the approach known as *utilitarianism*, pioneered by Jeremy Bentham (1748–1834) and later developed by John Stuart Mill (1806–1873). Utilitarianism is based on three principles.

1. *Measurable and interpersonally comparable utility.* The satisfaction that a person derives from the consumption of various goods and services can be aggregated into an index of her utility or welfare, and this index is comparable among persons. (This assumption underlies the notion of the utility possibilities set.)
2. *Welfarism.* The social evaluation of a state of the economy depends only on the levels of utility, or welfare, reached by individuals. In

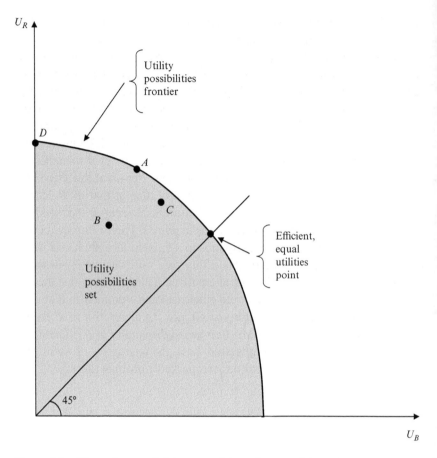

Figure 1.2   *The utility possibilities set and the utility possibilities frontier*

particular, it does not depend on the way the state is reached, or on the consumption of particular goods by each person.

3. *Society's welfare defined as the sum of utilities.* The aggregation, with equal weights, of the levels of utility or welfare reached by every person is the relevant index of social welfare. The weights in the aggregation must be the same for all individuals, because "each individual must count as one, and none as more than one."

Formally, in a society with a given number *I* of individuals, we define a *social welfare function* as a function of the vector of individual utilities. The values of the social welfare function are then interpreted as an index of society's welfare. Utilitarianism is then described by the social welfare function:[7]

$$W_U(U_1,\ldots,U_I) := U_1 + \ldots + U_I.$$

Utilitarianism is to some extent antiegalitarian, because it considers as socially indifferent a state where Person 1 attains the utility level 50,000 and the 999 remaining persons in society ($I = 1,000$) reach a level of zero, and another state where each of the 1,000 individuals reaches the utility level 50.[8] This feature of utilitarianism has motivated other notions of society's welfare that keep (1) and (2), but adopt alternative social welfare functions. If we define as *welfarist* a notion of the society's welfare that maintains principles (1) and (2), then these newer notions are special instances of the welfarism.

Within the welfarist approach, at the opposite end of utilitarianism we have the *maximin* (or *Rawlsian*) social welfare function, defined by

$$W_M(U_1,\ldots,U_I) := \min\{U_1,\ldots,U_I\},$$

which identifies social welfare with the utility of the worst-off person in society.[9] The maximin social welfare function is explicitly egalitarian, because maximizing the utility of the worst-off person will typically require the equalization of utilities.

---

[7] The symbol $:=$ means "is defined as."

[8] It must be said that classical utilitarians were actually egalitarians, because they coupled the maximization of the sum of utilities with the assumption of decreasing marginal utilities. In particular, they believed that the marginal utility of wealth, comparable among individuals, is decreasing. Hence, if a dollar is transferred from a wealthy person to a poor one, the utility loss of a wealthy person is lower, in absolute value, than the utility gain of the poor person, and the transfer increases the sum of utilities in society. As we will see below, in many of our examples utilitarianism does entail equal utilities.

[9] Named after John Rawls (1921–2002).

We may consider social welfare functions intermediate between utilitarianism and maximin. For instance, instead of adding utilities we could multiply them, yielding the social welfare function

$$W_N(U_1,\ldots,U_I) := U_1 \times U_2 \times \ldots \times U_I.$$

Because Nash proposed this expression for his solution to the bargaining problem, the function is often referred to as the *Nash* Social Welfare Function.

In terms of Figure 1.2, when moving along the utility possibilities frontier, one person's utility increases, and that of the other person decreases. The slope of the frontier gives the rate at which Red's utility decreases as that of Blue increases. Alternative social welfare functions evaluate the utility tradeoffs in different manners. Social welfare according to one such function is maximized at the point on the utility possibilities frontier where the highest possible social indifference curve (defined as a level curve of the given social welfare function) is reached.

1.5.2 Expensive and cheap tastes

Welfarism has been criticized because of its basic assumption of measurable, interpersonally comparable utilities. In actuality, however, we make many collective decisions taking into account the magnitudes of the welfare gains and losses of various people. True, modern *positive* economics does not require the measurability and interpersonal comparability of utility, but this does not imply that the notion is preposterous or that it cannot underpin normative recommendations.

Welfarism does suffer from more basic shortcomings. In particular, it does not distinguish between "wishes" and "needs:" this raises two problems, namely those of *expensive* and *cheap* tastes.

The expensive tastes problem goes as follows. Let Person *i* require more resources than Person *h* in order to reach a certain level of utility or welfare. The equalization of marginal utilities, as classical utilitarianism recommends, would imply that a large fraction of society's resources be devoted to Person *i*. Is that fair?

The modern answer, following the line pioneered by Rawls and developed by Amartya Sen and others, is that it depends on whether we are dealing with a need or not.[10] If *i* is a disabled person who needs abundant resources to achieve a minimal degree of mobility, then the answer may

---

[10] See A. Sen (1992), *Inequality Reexamined*, Cambridge, MA: Harvard University Press. Sen (born 1933) was awarded the Nobel Prize in Economic Sciences in 1998.

be Yes. At the other extreme, perhaps Person i has expensive tastes, and requires French champagne and Russian caviar to reach the same level of utility that Person h reaches with pork and beans. Social welfare criteria should be able to distinguish between these two situations, whereas utilitarianism, and more generally welfarism, does not take these distinctions into account.

The counterpart of the expensive tastes problem is that of cheap tastes, emphasized by Sen. These are tastes that have evolved under conditions of deprivation or limited opportunities, such as the tastes of "the battered slave, the hopeless destitute, the tamed housewife. . . ." Satisfying these tastes does not require large amount of resources, but it would be unfair to give them the same weight as those of people whose tastes have not been shaped by oppression or deprivation.

The problems of expensive and cheap tastes motivate explicitly considering the capacities that the various goods and services provide. Accordingly, the modern approach favors the supply of particular goods and services which are seen as important for enabling an adequate standard of living, such as health and education services. The characteristics of the goods supplied and their effects on the quality of life are then more relevant that the subjective levels of utility that they generate.

1.5.3   Equality of opportunity

For traditional welfarism, only the final outcomes count, measured in terms of individual utility or welfare. The modern vision attaches more weight to the way an outcome is reached, whether it is because of circumstances beyond a person's control or, on the contrary, as an effect of the person's actions. The modern conception of distributive justice departs from welfarism by postulating that:

1.   At a certain level, all persons have the same rights;
2.   Each person is responsible for the consequences of her actions;
3.   No person is to be held responsible for the effects, on her outcome, of circumstances that society deems to be beyond her control.

These ideas lead to the equality of opportunities as a social objective.

How can we make this idea precise? In principle, most people accept that a just society must seek to equalize opportunities. But different people understand equality of opportunity in different ways. One extreme position is to identify equality of opportunity with formal equality, i.e., with the absence of legal or administrative hurdles to access education and jobs, and with the imposition of meritocratic criteria for selection and promotion. Formal equality of opportunities excludes ethnic or gender discrimination, but it does not advocate any special measures to counteract disadvantages due to race, gender, or to the economic or social status of the family where one has been born. We would have, at the other extreme, equality of outcomes, aimed at eliminating any inequality in the situations where individuals find themselves.

Equality of opportunity is based on the idea of responsibility, i.e., on the distinction between the consequences of actions under the control of the person, and those due to circumstances outside a person's control. From this viewpoint, identifying equality of opportunities with formal equality amounts to making the person totally responsible for her situation. At the other extreme, outcome equality amounts to a certain determinism: no person is totally responsible for the situation in which she finds herself. Modern ideas of equality of opportunity try to avoid these extremes and search for practical criteria that make it possible to determine the scope of personal responsibility and deduce the implications of the principle of equality of opportunity for economic and social policies.

The principle of equality of opportunity can also be seen as an implication of *ex ante* efficiency, broadly understood (Chapter 6 below). Neutralizing inequalities due to circumstances outside a person's control can be seen as a way of compensating for the effects of bad luck in life's lottery.

1.6   Traditional economic postulates and economic efficiency

Pareto efficiency is a general notion, whereas we use the term *economic efficiency* in a more restricted manner: *economic efficiency* specializes Pareto efficiency to the case where two *traditional economics postulates* are adopted.[11] The first postulate is an assumption on what is feasible, and a second one on individual preferences.

First Traditional Economics Postulate: *Costless lumpsum transfers are feasible*. When defining efficiency, economics traditionally adopts a minimalist concept of feasibility: only resource and technology constraints are taken into account, while potential limitations due to institutions, property rights, or the availability of information are ignored. In particular, society has the capability to costlessly transfer goods or wealth among economic agents in any form: redistributions do not entail administrative or incentive costs, and *lumpsum transfers* (defined by the property that they are not

---

[11] Economic efficiency is sometimes called *allocative efficiency* or *first-best efficiency*.

influenced by individual behavior) are possible. In Arthur Okun's expression, the "transfer buckets" do not leak.[12]

The postulate of costless lumpsum transfers provides a useful benchmark, but is not particularly realistic, because it entails the existence of an agent of society (the "government") who is able to implement any allocation or reallocation of goods, and any productive activity, subject only to the physical laws imposed by production technologies and available resources. This is not always possible in actuality, among other reasons because often the most important asset owned by a person is her time, which cannot be directly transferred to another person (at least in nonslave societies). There may be indirect transfer methods, such as income taxes, but their scope is not universal, and they may be subject to incentive effects. In addition, the public sector may be unable to measure relevant characteristics of a person, such as her human capital, and the person may not wish to reveal information that can be used against her interests.

If the policy maker faces constraints beyond those admitted by the first traditional economics postulate, then the set of feasible alternatives is *smaller*, and some allocations or states that are not economically efficient (because they are Pareto dominated by an alternative that does satisfy the technology and resource constraints, but necessitates unfeasible redistributions) may be Pareto efficient given the smaller feasible set: such an allocation or state is called *second-best efficient*.

Second Traditional Economics Postulate: *The preferences of a person depend only on the final state of the economy, and are neutral with respect to procedure.* A person is only interested in the final state of the economy, and not in the manner in which it is attained, whether, say, she reaches a particular consumption bundle by her own efforts or by a charitable handout.

1.7 A simple model

This chapter considers a simple economy without externalities and without uncertainty. Externalities (resp. uncertainty) will be studied in Chapter 3 (resp. 6) below. As in Section 1.4.3 above, we postulate that there are only two persons, named Ms. Blue and Mr. Red.[13]

---

[12] A.M. Okun (1975), *Equality and Efficiency, the Big Tradeoff*, Washington, DC: Brookings Institution.

[13] The analysis can be easily extended to any finite number of people. Appendix 1A below indicates the required modifications for an indivisible good and an uncountable number of people.

1.7.1 Production and costs

We analyse the welfare effects of supplying a good or service, which we call good X. For instance, good X can be

- A *private good* like shoes, education or electricity: we write then x_B for the amount consumed by Blue, and x_R for the amount consumed by Red.
- A *public good*, such as TV programming, or a certain amount of information, available to both persons in the same amount x.

The default assumption is that the amounts of good X can in principle be any nonnegative real number. But we will on occasion consider a "Yes–No," or "dichotomous," private or public good, the amount of which made available to a person is either zero (for No) or one (for Yes).

We also assume that there is another good called the *numeraire*. This is a *nonproduced, transferable, desirable,* and *perfectly divisible* good interpreted as a proxy for all goods other than good X. The numeraire can be either consumed or used as an input in the production of X. The technology available in society is described by a (physical) *cost function*, denoted C. We interpret

$$C(\textit{Total amount of good X produced})$$

as the amount of numeraire socially needed to produce a given total amount of good X. We assume that $C(0) = 0$, interpreted as the absence of sunk costs.

The numeraire is initially available in the economy in the amount ω, called the *initial endowment of numeraire*. (Perhaps Blue and Red are initially endowed with ω_B and ω_R, respectively, and $\omega = \omega_B + \omega_R$.) Blue's and Red's final quantities of numeraire are denoted m_B and m_R respectively.

The inequality

$$\textit{Amount of numeraire available for consumption}$$

$$\leq \omega - C(\textit{Total amount of good X produced}), \tag{1.1}$$

defines the production possibilities in this economy.

As emphasized in Section 1.6 above, by defining feasibility by only the physical balance condition (1.1), we are admitting the feasibility of costless lumpsum transfers.

1.7.2   Preferences and utility

As specified in Section 1.4.3 above, each individual has a utility function which, in particular, represents her preferences. If good X is a private good not subject to externalities, Blue's and Red's utility functions are written $U_B(x_B, m_B)$ and $U_R(x_R, m_R)$, respectively. If good X is a public good, then the utility functions are written $U_B(x, m_B)$ and $U_R(x, m_R)$.

1.7.3   Allocations and efficiency

If good X is a private good, and there are two people in society (Blue and Red), a *feasible allocation* (or *feasible state* of the economy) is a list of four numbers x_B, m_B, x_R and m_R satisfying:

$$m_B + m_R + C(x_B + x_R) \leq \omega, \tag{1.2}$$

i.e.,

$$m_B + m_R \leq \omega - C(x_B + x_R),$$

which specializes inequality (1.1) to the case of private goods. Equality (1.2), for instance, reads: "Blue's and Red's consumption of numeraire plus the amount of numeraire used as an input in the production of good X (i.e., the sum of all the uses of the numeraire) cannot exceed the amount ω of numeraire available." This is a physical balance condition: an allocation for which "$m_B + m_R + C(x_B + x_R) > \omega$" is physically impossible.

If good X is a public good, then a feasible allocation or state is a list of three numbers x, m_B and m_R, satisfying

$$m_B + m_R + C(x) \leq \omega,$$

i.e.,

$$m_B + m_R \leq \omega - C(x), \tag{1.3}$$

which specializes inequality (1.1) to public goods.

When applied to our simple model, the notion of economic efficiency (see Section 1.6 above) reads as follows. An allocation (x_B, m_B, x_R, m_R) of a private-good economy which satisfies (1.2) (resp., a state (x, m_B, m_R) of a public-good economy which satisfies (1.3)) is *(economically) efficient* if there does not exist another feasible allocation or state satisfying (1.2) (resp. (1.3)) that everybody prefers to it or is indifferent to it, and at least one person prefers to it.

It follows from the definition that, at an economically efficient allocation, Red's utility level is the highest one consistent with feasibility as defined by (1.1), conditional to Blue's reaching at least the level of utility that she is reaching there.[14]

It immediately follows from the definition that we cannot have the strict inequality $m_B + m_R + C(x_B + x_R) < \omega$ at an efficient allocation: if we had, then some numeraire would be wasted that could be distributed to the consumers. Thus, in what follows we shall replace the weak inequality (1.2) by the equality

$$m_B + m_R + C(x_B + x_R) = \omega \quad \text{(if } X \text{ is a private good)} \qquad (1.4)$$

and the weak inequality (1.3) by the equality

$$m_B + m_R + C(x) = \omega \quad \text{(if } X \text{ is a public good)}. \qquad (1.5)$$

Condition (1.4) (or (1.5)), stating that no numeraire is wasted, is referred to as *production efficiency*, which is necessary, but not sufficient, for an allocation to be efficient.

As long as the utility functions are differentiable and all consumers consume positive amounts of all goods, a necessary condition for economic efficiency in the case of private goods not subject to externalities is the *equality of the marginal rates of substitution of all consumers*. This rules out the possibility of mutually beneficial exchanges between any two consumers. Obviously, economic efficiency would not hold if there were unexploited possibilities of mutually beneficial trades.[15]

1.8   Quasilinearity and surplus analysis

1.8.1   Valuation functions

The mathematics required to deal with efficient allocations in general falls beyond the scope of this book, and we will limit ourselves to a specific

---

[14] Mathematically, an efficient allocation maximizes Blue's utility subject to the physical balance constraint (1.1) and to the condition that Red reaches (at least) the utility level that he attains at that allocation. In other words, (for a private good) the allocation $(\bar{x}_B, \bar{m}_B, \bar{x}_R, \bar{m}_R)$ is efficient if and only if it maximizes $U_B(x_B, m_B)$ subject to $m_B + m_R + C(x_B + x_R) = \omega$ and to $U_R(x_R, m_R) = U_R(\bar{x}_R, \bar{m}_R)$.

[15] We will reencounter this condition as the equality of the marginal valuations in quasilinear economies (Section 2.1 below), and as the tangency condition in the Edgeworth boxes of Chapter 6.

type of preferences for which the problem becomes surprisingly simple, and in fact conceptually equivalent, for private-goods economies without externalities, to the pervasive notion of maximizing the sum of consumer surplus and producer surplus: see Section 2.4.5 below.

Let good X be a private good without externalities: the discussion can easily be extended to public goods and to externalities. Consider utility functions of the form

$$U_B(x_B, m_B) = \sqrt{v_B(x_B) + m_B},$$

$$U_R(x_R, m_R) = \sqrt{v_R(x_R) + m_R},$$

where $v_B(0) = v_R(0) = 0$. Observe that Blue's utility function is a (strictly) concave transformation of $v_B(x_B) + m_B$ (which we assume nonnegative). Whenever the utility function of Blue is a transformation of a function of the form $v_B(x_B) + m_B$, we say that Blue is, or her preferences are, *quasilinear*.[16]

We synonymously call $v_B(x_B)$:

*   The (total) *valuation* by Blue of x_B units of good X ;
*   The (total) *benefit* that Blue derives from x_B units of X ;
*   The (total) *willingness* of Blue *to pay* for x_B units of X, i.e., $v_B(x_B)$ is the maximum amount of numeraire that Blue is willing to give in exchange for x_B units of X;
*   The (total) *willingness* of Blue *to accept* for x_B units of X, i.e., if Blue had x_B units of good X in her possession, $v_B(x_B)$ would be the minimum amount of numeraire that she would accept for giving up her x_B units of X.

The "(total) willingness to pay" interpretation can be justified as follows. Let Blue have ω_B units of numeraire (a large number) to begin with, and let us offer her x_B units of X in exchange for T units of numeraire; if she takes the offer, then she ends up with x_B units of X and $(\omega_B - T)$ units of numeraire, with resulting utility $\sqrt{v_B(x_B) + \omega_B - T}$; if she refuses, then she ends up with zero units of X and ω_B units of numeraire, with resulting utility $\sqrt{v_B(0) + \omega_B} = \sqrt{\omega_B}$. She would accept the offer only if $T \leq v_B(x_B)$, i.e., $v_B(x_B)$ is the maximum amount she will be willing to pay for x_B units of X.

Accordingly, for $i = B, R$, the derivative $v_i'(x_i)$ is called i's *marginal valuation* function (or *marginal willingness-to-pay*, or *marginal benefit* function).

---

[16] We refer to Blue without loss of generality: of course, the remarks apply to Red and to any consumer.

The example that will be used most often in this book is the *quadratic valuation function*

$$v_i(x_i) = a_i x_i - 0.5 b_i [x_i]^2 + m_i,$$

($a_i > 0, b_i > 0$) for $i = B, R$, where amounts of x_i greater than a_i/b_i are typically disregarded, with marginal valuation

$$v_i'(x_i) = a_i - b_i x_i.$$

Thus, Consumer i's utility function is, in this case:

$$U_i(x_i, m_i) = \sqrt{a_i x_i - 0.5 b_i [x_i]^2 + m_i}.$$

It can be seen that the marginal utilities of both good X and the numeraire good are positive and decreasing.[17]

This formulation is valid when the consumption or production of good X creates no externalities. Otherwise, as we will study in Chapter 3, v_R, say, would have both x_B and x_R as variables. As before, when X is a public good, we write $x_B = x_R = x$.

Geometrically, if preferences are quasilinear, then the indifference curves (with the numeraire on the vertical axis) are vertically parallel: any two indifference curves are vertical translations of each other. It follows that the slope of any of Blue's indifference curves at a particular point (in other words, her marginal rate of substitution of the numeraire for good X at that point) depends only on the amount of good X (the horizontal coordinate of the point), and does not depend on the amount of numeraire (the vertical coordinate of the point). Indeed, all indifference curves have equations of the type

$$m_B = \text{constant} - v_B(x_B),$$

and the absolute value of the slope of the indifference curve at a point is simply $v_B'(x_B)$, Blue's marginal valuation of the amount x_B of good X.

Quasilinearity is our default assumption. We also assume that all allocations satisfy (1.4) or (1.5).

---

[17] Quasilinearity is not a realistic assumption: it implies that Blue's demand for good X is independent of her wealth (income): i.e., good X is borderline normal-inferior. If Blue's preferences were not quasilinear, then her "valuation" of x_B or "willingness to pay" for x_B would depend on her wealth or on her consumption of numeraire. Surplus analysis would then not be exact, although it could still be used as an approximation.

1.8.2   Social surplus

In our quasilinear world we can give a particular meaning to the notion of "size of the social pie," for which we use the term *social surplus* by aggregating valuations (willingness to pay) over individuals and subtracting total cost, i.e.,

$$Social\ surplus := Sum\ of\ valuations - Cost.$$

The precise definitions are as follows.

Definition (private goods, no externalities). The *social surplus* of (or generated by) the pair of quantities (x_B, x_R) is

$$S(x_B, x_R) := v_B(x_B) + v_R(x_R) - C(x_B + x_R). \qquad (1.6)$$

Definition (public goods). The *social surplus* of (or generated by) the quantity x of the public good is

$$S(x) := v_B(x) + v_R(x) - C(x). \qquad (1.7)$$

As an example, let good X be a Yes–No public project, say, a species conservation program. Social surplus when the program is undertaken is:

$$S(1) = v_B(1) + v_R(1) - C(1).$$

Otherwise, social surplus is $S(0) = v_B(0) + v_R(0) - C(0) = 0$. Now, depending on people's preferences and on the cost function, it may happen that $S(1) > 0$ or that $S(1) < 0$. When $S(1) > 0$ one may say that the "size of the pie" is larger with the program than without it, whereas, if $S(1) < 0$, then not implementing the program yields the largest pie. This notion of the "size of the pie" will be justified in the following sections.

1.8.3   Efficiency and the maximization of social surplus

Efficiency has a simple characterization if preferences are quasilinear.

Fact (Quasilinear preferences). A feasible allocation or state that uses up all the numeraire is efficient if and only if the level of surplus that it generates is at least as large as that of any other feasible allocation.[18]

---

[18] Strictly speaking, the necessity of surplus maximization should be qualified with the proviso that everybody has sufficiently large amounts of numeraire,

The fact can be rephrased as follows. *A feasible allocation is efficient if and only if it maximizes social surplus over all feasible allocations (that do not waste numeraire).* Appendix 1C provides a formal proof. Intuitive arguments for the cases of private and public goods are provided in Chapters 2 and 4, respectively. They can easily be extended to economies with externalities.

We call the difference between the maximal surplus given the technological and resource constraints and the magnitude of surplus actually achieved at an inefficient allocation the *deadweight loss* of the allocation.

1.8.4   The maximization of a social welfare function

As noted in Section 1.5.1 above, the maximization of the maximin, or Rawlsian, social welfare function implies equal utilities. It turns out that, for the utility functions of this section, the maximization of any (symmetrical) social welfare functions also implies equal utilities.[19] Hence, all these social welfare functions choose the point, in Figure 1.2 where the utility possibilities frontier intersects the 45° line.

---

or that the numbers m_B and m_R could be negative. We disregard this technical point.

[19] This follows from the fact that we apply the same, strictly concave transformation to $v_i + m_i$, where v_i is a function of the x variables, but not of the numeraire variables. Consider a society with I persons: the utility function of Person i is $f(v_i + m_i)$, with $f' > 0$ and $f'' < 0$. The maximization of the utilitarian social welfare function $\Sigma_{i=1}^{I} f(v_i + m_i)$ subject to $\Sigma_{i=1}^{I} m_i = \omega - C$ can be written max $\Sigma_{i=1}^{I-1} f(v_i + m_i) + f(v_I + \omega - C - \Sigma_{i=1}^{I-1} m_i)$. The first-order condition for m_i is $f'(v_i + m_i) = f'(v_I + m_I)$, which implies equal utilities by the strict concavity of f.

Appendix 1A   A Yes–No good with a continuum of people

1A.1   A continuum economy

There is a continuum $(0, N_0]$ of people: think of each of them as being named by a real number in the interval $(0, N_0]$ (perhaps they are named by a social security number, which can be an infinite decimal). We have our usual two goods: good X and the numeraire. The numeraire is, as in the main text, a private, desirable and divisible good, initially available in society in the amount ω. But now good X is a Yes–No, or "dichotomous" good. A given person can either have access to it (her consumption or use is then one) or not (zero).

We call a person in the interval $(0, N_0]$ a *potential consumer* or *potential user, of good X*, and, if good X is made available to her, then we say that she is an *(actual) consumer* or *user*. For reasons that will become clear, we consider only situations where the set of actual consumers is an interval of the form $(0, N]$, where $N \leq N_0$, i.e., whenever a person consumes good X, anybody with a lower number also does. We then call N the *consumption level*, and let $N = 0$ when nobody consumes good X. We interpret N/N_0 as the *fraction of actual consumers*.[20]

As usual, the numeraire good can be used as an input in the production of good X, according to the technology defined by the cost function $C(N)$. When $N > 0$, $C(N)$ is the cost of providing one unit of good X to each person in the interval $(0, N]$, and $C(0)$ denotes the cost of not producing the good at all, assumed to be zero, i.e., $C(0) = 0$.[21]

A *feasible allocation* is defined by a consumption level N of good X and a function $m(n)$ indicating the consumption of the numeraire good by each potential consumer $n \in (0, N_0]$. The allocation is feasible if

$$\int_0^{N_0} m(n)\,dn + C(N) \leq \omega. \tag{1A.1}$$

---

[20] One may be tempted to call N the "number of actual consumers," or N_0 the "number of potential consumers," but this is mathematically incorrect, because there is an uncountable infinity of points in the interval $(0, N]$ (for $N > 0$). Of course, we could adopt an alternative, finite model with an integer number N_0 of potential consumers (i.e., with the finite set $\{1, 2, \ldots, N_0\}$ as the set of consumers), but it would actually be more cumbersome, involving inequalities at the margin, and facing difficulties in the interpretation of fractional solutions.

[21] Here we adopt the interpretation that there no consumer is named 0, so that $N = 0$ means "nobody." Because a single point is negligible in the continuum, we could consider $[0, N_0]$, instead of $(0, N_0]$, as the set of potential consumers. We postulate in any event that all relevant functions are defined (and integrable) on the interval $[0, N_0]$.

Compare with (1.1) above: because now we aggregate over a continuum of consumers, the mathematical operation required is integration rather than addition.

In this appendix, as in appendices 2A and 5A below, we consider the case of a private good not subject to externalities. Continuum economies with externalities (resp. public goods) are covered in Appendix 3A (resp. Appendix 4A).

1A.2   Valuations, surplus and efficiency

We maintain the quasilinearity assumption. People have different valuations of good X: we denote by $\bar{v}(n)$ the valuation of (one unit of) good X by Person $n \in (0, N_0]$ Accordingly, Person n's utility is:

* $\sqrt{\bar{v}(n)} + m$ if she has access to good X and to m units of the numeraire good;
* $\sqrt{m}$ if she does not have access to good X, but has access to m units of the numeraire good.

People are ordered in the interval $(0, N_0]$ *by valuation*: the higher a person's number, the lower (or at least, not higher) her valuation. Formally, if $n_1 > n_0$, then $\bar{v}(n_1) \le \bar{v}(n_0)$, or, in other words, the function $\bar{v}(n)$ of individual valuations is non-increasing. The curve labeled $\bar{v}(n)$ in Figure 1A.1 illustrates this assumption: people with a high number n have zero valuation of the good, and for the others, individual valuations are actually decreasing with n. Our postulate that the set of actual consumers is an interval $(0, N]$ then means that actual consumers are those who value the good the most, or that there is "efficient rationing."

We now define the *social surplus function* $S(N)$ as

$$S(N) := \int_0^N \bar{v}(n)\,\mathrm{d}n - C(N) \tag{1A.2}$$

(compare with (1.6) above). In line with our analysis in Section 1.8.3 above, we characterize economic efficiency by the conditions of surplus maximization and the absence of numeraire waste (i.e., (1A.1) must be satisfied with equality). Differentiating (1A.2) with respect to N (apply the Fundamental Theorem of Calculus) and setting the derivative equal to zero yields the first order condition for surplus maximization

$$\bar{v}(N) = C'(N),$$

which can be read as:

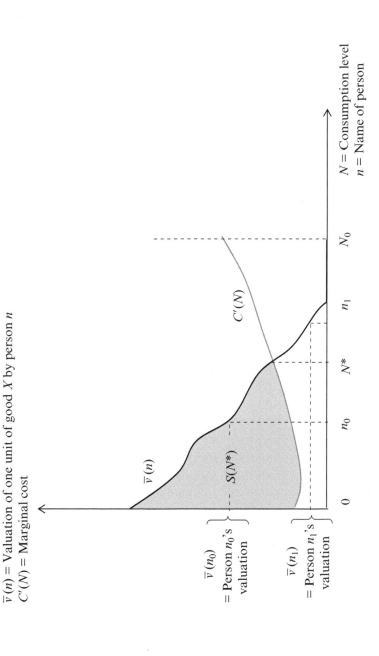

Figure 1A.1 *Individual valuations and surplus maximization in the continuum economy*

Valuation of the Marginal Consumer = Marginal cost.

This is illustrated in Figure 1A.1, which combines the individual valuations function with the marginal cost function $C'(N)$. The intersection of the two curves gives the consumption level N^* compatible with economic efficiency. The consumer with name N^* is the marginal consumer, and her valuation of good X, $\bar{v}(N^*)$, equals the marginal cost $C'(N^*)$, which can be interpreted as the rate at which society's cost increases in order to provide good X to the marginal consumer.

Appendix IB   Game theory

Strategic interaction is often modeled as a (noncooperative) game in economics, other social sciences, and evolutionary biology. Some important examples are:

1. Cournot oligopoly.
2. Prisoner's dilemma.
3. Evolutionary stability.

In this book we will encounter the following examples.

4. The tragedy of the commons in the version presented below in this appendix.
5. The Hotelling model of the two ice-cream sellers on the beach defined as the interval [0, 1] (Section 4.3.2.5 below).
6. The Hotelling–Downs model of the political competition on the one-dimensional policy interval [0, 1] (Section 4.3.2.5 below).
7. Voluntary contributions (Section 4.4 below).

Formally, a game (in normal or strategic form) is specified by:

- The list of decision makers or *players*, denoted $1, \ldots, I$. For examples 1 to 7, they are interpreted as follows.
  - Example 1: oligopolistic firms.
  - Example 2: prisoners ($I = 2$).
  - Example 3: individuals of a given species or genotypes.
  - Example 4: villagers ($I = 2$).
  - Example 5: ice-cream sellers ($I = 2$).
  - Example 6: political parties ($I = 2$).
  - Example 7: citizens.
- For each Player $i = 1, \ldots, I$, a set of *strategies*, i.e., decisions or plans of action, available to her. The strategies in examples 1 to 7 are interpreted as follows.
  - Example 1: the set of strategies is the real interval $[0, \infty)$, where a number is interpreted as either the quantity of output that the firm brings to the market, or the price that the firm charges.
  - Example 2: each prisoner has only two strategies, namely "confess" and "do not confess."
  - Example 3: possible behaviors, such as "fight" or "flight."
  - Example 4: the number of cows that a villager takes to graze on the commons.
  - Example 5: locations on the beach.

- ○ Example 6: positions on the one-dimensional political spectrum.
  - ○ Example 7: contributions to the supply of a public good.
- For each Player $i = 1,\ldots, I$, a *payoff* function, that expresses the level of welfare or benefit achieved by Player i and has as arguments the strategies played by everybody. The payoffs in the previous examples can be interpreted as follows.
  - ○ Example 1: profits.
  - ○ Example 2: minus the number of years that the prisoner gets.
  - ○ Example 3: evolutionary fitness.
  - ○ Example 4: milk output.
  - ○ Example 5: quantity of ice cream sold.
  - ○ Example 6: probability of winning the election.
  - ○ Example 7: valuation of the amount of the public good minus the contribution.

There are two notions of noncooperative equilibrium: a stricter one, named *dominant strategy equilibrium*, and a weaker one, named *Cournot–Nash equilibrium.*[22] The dominant strategy equilibrium concept is stricter in the sense that a dominant strategy equilibrium is automatically a Cournot–Nash equilibrium, but a Cournot–Nash equilibrium may or may not be a dominant strategy equilibrium.

Definition. A combination of strategies, one for each player, is called a *Cournot–Nash equilibrium* if the strategy played by any given player yields her a higher (or at least no lower) payoff than any other of the strategies available to her, *when all the other players play their equilibrium strategies.*

Definition. A combination of strategies, one for each player, is called a *(strictly) dominant strategy equilibrium* if the strategy played by any given player yields her a higher payoff than any other of the strategies available to her *no matter what other players play* (*whether they play their equilibrium strategies, or any other strategy*).

Most games have a Cournot–Nash equilibrium, but only very special games have a dominant strategy equilibrium. In our list, only games 2 and 4 have a dominant strategy equilibrium.

A Cournot-Nash equilibrium can also be characterized in terms of *best replies*. A strategy is a best reply of a player to the strategies of the other players if it maximizes her payoff given the strategies of the other players. We can then say that a Cournot–Nash equilibrium is a

---

[22] A Cournot–Nash equilibrium is sometimes called a Nash equilibrium, or a Nash noncooperative equilibrium.

combination of strategies with the property that each player is playing a best reply to the strategies played by the other players.

For formal definitions, it is convenient to adopt a notation that distinguishes between the strategy played by Player i, denoted σ_i, and the strategies played by the other players, denoted $(\sigma_1, \sigma_2, \ldots, \sigma_{i-1}, \sigma_{i+1} \ldots, \sigma_I)$ or σ_{-i} for short (i.e., σ_{-i} has $I - 1$ components). We denote Player i's payoff function by $\Pi_i(\sigma_i, \sigma_{-i})$.

Definition. A tuple of strategies $(\tilde{\sigma}_1, \tilde{\sigma}_2, \ldots, \tilde{\sigma}_I)$, one for each player, is a *Cournot–Nash equilibrium* if, for $i = 1, \ldots, I$, $\Pi_i(\tilde{\sigma}_i; \tilde{\sigma}_{-i}) \geq \Pi_i(\sigma_i, \tilde{\sigma}_{-i})$, for all σ_i.

Definition. A tuple of strategies $(\tilde{\sigma}_1, \tilde{\sigma}_2, \ldots, \tilde{\sigma}_I)$, one for each player, is a (*strictly*) *dominant strategy equilibrium* if, for $i = 1, \ldots, I$, $\Pi_i(\tilde{\sigma}_i, \sigma_{-i}) > \Pi_i(\sigma_i, \sigma_{-i})$, for all σ_i and for all σ_{-i}.

We now consider a simple example inspired by Garrett Hardin's "tragedy of the commons."[23] (See Section 3A.2 below for discussion and for a different model.) There are two villagers, each of whom can take to the common grazing range either six or eight cows: these are the only two strategies available to each player. But the more cows in the range, the more scarce the grass, and the lower the milk output per cow, postulated to equal 24 minus the number of grazing cows. The payoffs (in gallons of milk) are described in Table 1B.1: that of Villager 1 (resp. 2) in the southwest (resp. northeast) corner of the corresponding cell.

The pair of strategies (8 cows, 8 cows) is the unique dominant strategy (and Cournot–Nash) equilibrium. If you are Villager 1 and if Villager 2 brings six cows, you are better off bringing eight cows (80 gallons vs. 72), and if Villager 2 brings eight cows, you are also better off bringing eight cows (64 gallons vs. 60). The equilibrium is Pareto inefficient: if each villager brought only six cows, each would obtain eight more gallons than at the equilibrium.

As noted above, few games have a dominant strategy equilibrium: they are the exception rather than the rule. Other versions of the "tragedy of the commons" fail to have a dominant strategy equilibrium, but they do have a Cournot–Nash equilibrium. But the equilibrium is inefficient in all versions, motivating the expression "tragedy," see 3A.2 in Chapter 3 below.

---

[23] The example is formally similar to the popular prisoner's dilemma.

Table 1B.1 *The two-villager, two-strategy tragedy of the commons*

Villager 1		Villager 2			
		6 cows		8 cows	
6 cows	72		72		80
			60		60
8 cows	80		60		64
			64		64

Appendix IC   Proof of the equivalence between efficiency and the maximization of surplus

Fact. Assume that the preferences of all consumers are quasilinear. An allocation that does not waste any numeraire is efficient if and only if the level of surplus that it generates is at least as large as that of any other feasible allocation.[24]

Proof. We start from footnote 14 above, which reads (for a private good): the allocation $(\overline{x}_B, \overline{m}_B, \overline{x}_R, \overline{m}_R)$ is efficient if and only if it "maximizes $U_B(x_B, m_B)$ subject to

$$m_B + m_R + C(x_B + x_R) = \omega \text{ and to } U_R(x_R, m_R) = U_R(\overline{x}_R, \overline{m}_R)."$$

For quasilinear preferences, and recalling that, for $i = B, R$, Person i's utility function is an increasing transformation of $v_i(x_i) + m_i$, this can be written:

"$(\overline{x}_B, \overline{m}_B, \overline{x}_R, \overline{m}_R)$ maximizes $v_B(x_B) + m_B$ subject to

$$m_B + m_R + C(x_B + x_R) = \omega, \tag{1C.1}$$

$$v_R(x_R) + m_R = v_R(\overline{x}_R) + \overline{m}_R." \tag{1C.2}$$

The constraint (1C.1) implies $m_B = \omega - m_R - C(x_B + x_R)$, which using the constraint (1C.2) yields $m_B = \omega - [v_R(\overline{x}_R) + \overline{m}_R - v_R(x_R)] - C(x_b + x_R)$. Hence, the maximization can be written: "$(\overline{x}_B, \overline{m}_B, \overline{x}_R, \overline{m}_R)$ maximizes

$$v_B(x_B) + \omega - v_R(\overline{x}_R) - \overline{m}_R - v_R(x_R) - C(x_B + x_R),"$$

which, because $\omega - v_R(\overline{x}_R) - \overline{m}_R$ is a constant, is equivalent to

"$(\overline{x}_B, \overline{m}_B, \overline{x}_R, \overline{m}_R)$ maximizes $v_B(x_B) + v_R(x_R) - C(x_B + x_R),"$

i.e.,

"$(\overline{x}_B, \overline{m}_B, \overline{x}_R, \overline{m}_R)$ maximizes $S(x_B, x_R)."$

The cases of externalities or public goods are similarly proven.

---

[24] The proof evidences that the necessity of surplus maximization for efficiency should be qualified with the proviso that everybody has sufficiently large amounts of numeraire, or that the numbers m_B and m_R could be negative, as indicated in footnote 18 above. The sufficiency of surplus maximization for efficiency does not require this qualification. The same remarks apply to Appendix 1D below.

Appendix 1D   The potential compensation criterion

Suppose that we start at some allocation and we move to another one. Such a move may benefit both people (we then say that the move is a *Pareto improvement*, or that the new allocation *Pareto dominates* the old one), or perhaps hurt both people, or benefit one person (the winner) and hurt another one (the loser). In the third case we say that the new allocation is *better than the previous one in the sense of the potential compensation criterion* (or the *potential improvement criterion,* or the *compensation principle*) if, after the move, the winner could transfer some numeraire to the loser in such a way that they both end up better off than before the move. (We also apply these expressions to actual Pareto improvements.) The following fact can be proved in a manner parallel to Appendix 1C.

Fact. (Quasilinear preferences). A feasible allocation is better than another one in the sense of the potential compensation criterion if and only if it generates a larger social surplus.

2 Private goods without externalities

• •

2.1 Efficiency conditions for private-goods economies without externalities

We return to the quasilinear economy of private goods without externalities presented in Section 1.8 of Chapter 1 above. Recall that its data are as follows:

Ms. Blue's utility function: $U_B(x_B, m_B) = \sqrt{v_B(x_B)} + m_B$, with $v_B(0) = 0$;

Mr. Red's utility function: $U_R(x_R, m_R) = \sqrt{v_R(x_R)} + m_R$, with $v_R(0) = 0$;

Social cost function: $C(x_B + x_R)$, with $C(0) = 0$;

Initial endowment of numeraire: ω.

The *social surplus* for this economy is defined in (1.6) above as

$$S(x_B, x_R) := v_B(x_B) + v_R(x_R) - C(x_B + x_R). \tag{2.1}$$

If all functions are differentiable, and if the maximization of social surplus occurs at point where both x_B and x_R are positive, then the maximization of (2.1) requires that the partial derivatives of social surplus with respect to x_B and to x_R be zero, i.e.,

$$v_B'(x_B) = C'(x_B + x_R), \tag{2.2}$$

and

$$v_R'(x_R) = C'(x_B + x_R). \tag{2.3}$$

These equalities have an intuitive interpretation. Suppose that (2.2) does not hold. If, say $v_B'(x_B) > C'(x_B + x_R)$, then producing some extra amount of good X and giving it to Blue would increase the sum of the valuations at the rate $v_B'(x_B)$, while increasing the cost at the lower rate $C'(x_B + x_R)$, resulting in a net gain in social surplus. Hence, surplus cannot be maximized at an allocation that violates (2.2).

And if $v_B'(x_B) > C'(x_B + x_R)$, then a Pareto-dominating allocation

could be found where Blue parts with a small amount of numeraire, which
is used to increase the production of good X, with Blue receiving the extra
amount of good X. Because $v'_B(x_B) > C'(x_B + x_R)$, Blue prefers the new
allocation, whereas Red's consumption bundle remains unchanged. It
follows that an allocation where (2.2) is not satisfied is not efficient.

Note that (2.2) and (2.3) imply that

$$v'_B(x_B) = v'_R(x_R),$$

which in quasilinear economies is precisely the condition of the equality of
the marginal rates of substitution mentioned in Section 1.7.3 of Chapter 1
above. Recall that it precludes the possibility of mutually beneficial trades
between any two consumers.

In summary, conditions (2.2) and (2.3) imply both *economic efficiency*
and the *maximization of surplus*, illustrating the equivalence between the
two discussed in Section 1.8.3 and Appendix 1C of Chapter 1 above.

2.2 The utility possibilities frontier

Consider the private-good case. A feasible allocation $(\bar{x}_B, \bar{m}_B, \bar{x}_R, \bar{m}_R)$
induces a utility level for Blue, namely $\bar{U}_B := U_B(\bar{x}_B, \bar{m}_B)$, and one for Red,
namely $\bar{U}_R := U_R(\bar{x}_R, \bar{m}_R)$: in other words, it induces a point $(\bar{U}_B, \bar{U}_R)$ in
the utility possibilities set, see Section 1.4.3 above. As seen there, the utility
point $(\bar{U}_B, \bar{U}_R)$ that corresponds to the allocation $(\bar{x}_B, \bar{m}_B, \bar{x}_R, \bar{m}_R)$ lies on
the utility possibilities frontier if and only if $(\bar{x}_B, \bar{m}_B, \bar{x}_R, \bar{m}_R)$ is an efficient
allocation. We shall then also say that $(\bar{U}_B, \bar{U}_R)$ is an efficient utility point
or pair.

The utility possibilities set can easily be constructed for our specification of the utility functions. Suppose that we fix the amounts of good
X available to Blue and Red, say at $\bar{x}_B$ and $\bar{x}_R$ units respectively. This
leaves an amount $\omega - C(\bar{x}_B + \bar{x}_R)$ of numeraire that can be distributed
in various ways between Blue and Red: if Blue gets m_B, then Red gets
$\omega - C(\bar{x}_B + \bar{x}_R) - m_B$. Each of these distributions yields a point (U_B, U_R)
in the utility possibilities set. What does the set of all such points, for fixed
$\bar{x}_B$ and $\bar{x}_R$, look like? Clearly

$$U_B = \sqrt{v_B(\bar{x}_B)} + m_B,$$

and

$$U_R = \sqrt{v_R(\bar{x}_R)} + \omega - C(\bar{x}_B + \bar{x}_R) - m_B.$$

Squaring both sides of the two equalities, and adding up, we obtain

$$[U_B]^2 + [U_R]^2 = v_B(\overline{x}_B) + v_R(\overline{x}_R) + \omega - C(\overline{x}_B + \overline{x}_R). \qquad (2.4)$$

Now $v_B(\overline{x}_B) + v_R(\overline{x}_R) - C(\overline{x}_B + \overline{x}_R) = S(\overline{x}_B, \overline{x}_R) := \overline{S}$, the social surplus achieved at $(\overline{x}_B, \overline{x}_R)$. Thus (2.4) can be written

$$[U_B]^2 + [U_R]^2 = \overline{S} + \omega.$$

Geometrically, the set of points in utility space (U_B, U_R) reached by keeping $\overline{x}_B$ and $\overline{x}_R$ fixed, and distributing the available numeraire in all conceivable manners is (an arc of) a circle centered at zero with radius $\sqrt{\overline{S} + \omega}$. Let us call it the *utility minifrontier for* $(\overline{x}_B, \overline{x}_R)$. See Figure 2.1.[1]

It follows that the utility minifrontiers corresponding to different pairs $(\overline{x}_B, \overline{x}_R)$ never cross. If $S(x_B^1, x_R^1) > S(x_B^0, x_R^0)$, then the utility minifrontier for (x_B^1, x_R^1) lies outside (above) the one for (x_B^0, x_R^0), because it has a larger radius. The outermost minifrontier is the one for the pair (x_B^*, x_R^*) that maximizes social surplus: its radius is $\sqrt{S^* + \omega}$, where S^* is the level of surplus achieved at (x_B^*, x_R^*), i.e., $S^* := S(x_B^*, x_R^*) \geq S(x_B, x_R)$ for all (x_B, x_R). This outermost minifrontier obviously coincides with the (grand) utility possibilities frontier of the economy.

Figure 2.1 provides a geometric proof of the fact stated in Section 1.8.3 and proved in Appendix 1C above: in our quasilinear world, the maximization of social surplus is equivalent to economic efficiency.

2.3   The First Fundamental Theorem of Welfare Economics and market failures

2.3.1   *The invisible hand and the theorem*

The theorem makes precise the old idea that free trade improves society's welfare. It is often attributed to Adam Smith (1723–1790), who employed the metaphor of the "invisible hand." In his words:[2]

---

[1] The frontiers are drawn as going all the way to the axes. Strictly speaking, this requires that $m_B < 0$ (resp., $m_R < 0$) for points of the frontier close to the vertical (resp. horizontal) axis. We disregard this technical point and draw the frontiers from axis to axis.

[2] A. Smith (1776), *An Inquiry into the Nature and Causes of the Wealth of Nations*, London: W. Strahan and T. Cadell, Paragraph IV.2.9.

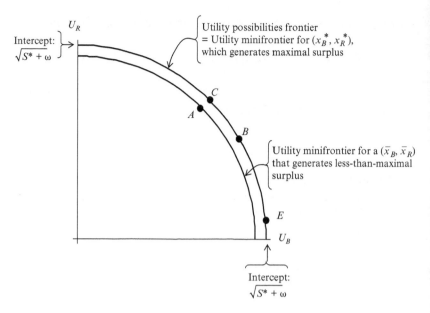

Figure 2.1   *Utility minifrontiers and the utility possibilities frontier*

As every individual, therefore, endeavours as much as he can both to employ his capital in the support of domestic industry, and so to direct that industry that its produce may be of the greatest value; every individual necessarily labours to render the annual revenue of the society as great as he can. He generally, indeed, neither intends to promote the public interest, nor knows how much he is promoting it. By preferring the support of domestic to that of foreign industry, he intends only his own security; and by directing that industry in such a manner as its produce may be of the greatest value, he intends only his own gain, and he is in this, as in many other cases, led by an invisible hand to promote an end which was no part of his intention. Nor is it always the worse for the society that it was no part of it. By pursuing his own interest he frequently promotes that of the society more effectually than when he really intends to promote it.

The meaning of this, by now famous, paragraph has been the subject of debate among historians of economic thought. In any event, as explained in Section 2.3.3 below, the smooth operation of markets does not guarantee the promotion of the "public interest" or "society's interest" beyond economic efficiency. It is the connection between markets and efficiency that is made precise by the First Fundamental Theorem of Welfare Economics, which can be stated as follows.

First Fundamental Theorem of Welfare Economics
Under the following conditions:

1. *Absence of externalities,*
2. *Absence of public goods,*
3. *Symmetrical (not necessarily perfect) information,*

the allocation obtained at a <u>general</u> <u>competitive</u> <u>equilibrium</u> is efficient.
The three underlined terms can be understood as adding the following qualifications:

4. *Competitive* markets. Not any market will do: the market must be perfectly competitive or, in other words, no market participant may have market power. This excludes monopolies, oligopolies and other imperfections of competition.
5. *Nonincreasing returns* to scale. This qualification is related to the previous one: as we will see in Chapter 5 below, we cannot have competitive markets if returns to scale are forever increasing. Any market equilibrium would in this case be imperfectly competitive.
6. *General* equilibrium. Requires *complete* financial and insurance *markets.*
7. *Equilibrium* allocations. Disequilibrium allocations, such as the ones resulting in unemployment, are typically not efficient.

2.3.2   Market failures

When any of conditions 1–7 is not satisfied, the First Fundamental Theorem of Welfare Economics does not apply.[3] It may occur that the affected markets still operate, but in an inefficient manner, or that some markets do not operate at all. These conditions may be interrelated: for instance, the incompleteness of markets (condition 6) may be due to asymmetrical information (condition 3), or to the presence of nonexcludable public goods (condition 2), and the lack of perfect competition (condition 4) may be due to increasing returns (condition 5).

The above conditions suggest a list of reasons for inefficiency, usually referred to as *market failures*, namely:

1. Externalities;
2. Public goods;
3. Asymmetrical information;
4. Imperfect competition;
5. Increasing returns to scale;
6. Incomplete markets;
7. Unemployment.

Each market failure motivates a class of government policies with primarily allocative objectives. For instance, in order to address market failure 4, the government may remove trade barriers, engage in antitrust policies against collusion, some mergers or predatory pricing. Market failures 1 and 2 will be extensively studied in chapters 3 and 4, respectively. Market failure 5 motivates the regulation of natural monopolies, studied in Chapter 5 below, whereas asymmetrical information 3 and its effects on market failure 6 are covered in Chapter 6.

2.3.3   Equity, efficiency and public policy

The First Fundamental Theorem of Welfare Economics guarantees that, when its conditions are satisfied, the allocation obtained at a competitive equilibrium satisfies the normative criterion of efficiency. But the theorem says nothing about the equity, or lack of it, of the allocation. Under the conditions of the theorem, the equilibrium allocation corresponds to a utility pair on the utility possibility frontier of Figure 2.1, but the actual point reached may well depend on the initial distribution of wealth. If, say, Blue is markedly wealthier than Red, then market equilibrium may

---

[3] The theorem, a statement of the form "if. . ., then. . .," is of course still true: theorems are true by definition.

lead to a point such as E in Figure 2.1, where Red reaches a very low level of utility. Market outcomes may be inequitable even when the First Fundamental Theorem applies, and there is no guarantee that any sensible social welfare function is maximized there. Joan Robinson (1903–1983) pushed Adam Smith's metaphor one step further when she wrote that "the hidden hand will always do its work, but it may work by strangulation."[4] This is the way that Red would feel if competitive markets led to point E in Figure 2.1, the efficiency of the allocation providing little comfort to him.

Market failures, as listed by the conditions of the First Fundamental Theorem of Welfare Economics, provide an efficiency rationale for some government policies. But some other policies are motivated by the equity criterion. And frequently both equity and efficiency considerations underpin public policies such as education or social insurance.

2.4 Surplus analysis of competitive markets

2.4.1 The First Fundamental Theorem in quasilinear economies

Under competitive market conditions, all consumers and firms take as given the market price p of good X (we set the price of the numeraire good equal to one). Let us return to our two quasilinear consumers without externalities, where:

Ms. Blue's utility function: $U_B(x_B, m_B) = \sqrt{v_B(x_B)} + m_B$, with $v_B(0) = 0$;

Mr. Red's utility function: $U_R(x_R, m_R) = \sqrt{v_R(x_R)} + m_R$, with $v_R(0) = 0$;

Social cost function: $C(x_B + x_R)$, with $C(0) = 0$.

Given the market price p, Blue chooses (x_B, m_B) in order to maximize $\sqrt{v_B(x_B)} + m_B$ subject to the constraint that $p\,x_B + m_B$ equal her wealth, a magnitude that she takes as given (it is in fact determined by the value of her endowments and her share in the profits of firms). Hence, she chooses x_B in order to maximize $v_B(x_B) - px_B$. At a maximum where she does not exhaust her wealth, the derivative of this expression must be zero, i.e.,

$$v_B'(x_B) = p. \tag{2.5}$$

4 J. Robinson (1946–1947), "The pure theory of international trade," *Review of Economic Studies*, 14(2), 98–112.

Similarly, for Red:

$$v_R'(x_R) = p.$$

In a parallel manner, each firm chooses its output level in order to maximize profits at price p, implying that its marginal cost equals p.

At a competitive equilibrium, the aggregate output of firms equals the aggregate demand by consumers, namely $x_B + x_R$. Because each firm's marginal cost equals the market price, p also equals the social marginal cost $C'(x_B + x_R)$, i.e.,

$$C'(x_B + x_R) = p.$$

Hence, the efficiency conditions of (2.2) and (2.3) above are satisfied, illustrating the First Fundamental Theorem.[5]

2.4.2   Obtaining valuation from demand

The function $v_B'(x_B)$ is Blue's *marginal valuation of* x_B, and also Blue's *inverse* (or indirect) *demand function*. By (2.5), if we observe Blue's market choices for each market price p, then we observe her marginal valuation function $v_B'(x_B)$.[6] We can compute Blue's (total) valuation $v_B(x_B)$ if we know her demand function (and we know that her preferences are quasilinear) as follows. The Fundamental Theorem of Calculus implies that $\int_0^{\overline{x}_B} v_B'(x_B)\,dx_B = v_B(\overline{x}_B) - v_B(0) = v_B(\overline{x}_B)$, i.e., *Blue's (total) valuation of* $\overline{x}_B$ *units of good X equals the area under her demand curve up to* $\overline{x}_B$.

For an illustration, let Ms. Blue's utility function be:

$$U_B(x_B, m_B) = \sqrt{a_B x_B - 0.5 b_B [x_B]^2} + m_B,$$

i.e., $v_B(x_B) = a_B x_B - 0.5 b_B [x_B]^2$. Therefore, her demand function is given by

$$p = a_B - b_B x_B,$$

or $x_B = [a_B - p]/b_B$, see Figure 2.2. Suppose that we do not know $v_B(x_B)$ but that we observe her demand curve $p = a_B - b_B x_B$. Then, in order to

---

[5] The production efficiency condition $m_B + m_R + C(x_B + x_R) = \omega$ (see (1.4) in Chapter 1 above) follows from the consumers' budget constraints, which when aggregated over consumers imply that [Aggregate value of consumption] = [Aggregate wealth] = [Aggregate endowment of numeraire] + [Aggregate profits], i.e., $m_B + m_R + p[x_B + x_R] = \omega + p[x_B + x_R] - C(x_B + x_R)$.

[6] Note that her demand for good X depends on p, but not on her wealth: this is a consequence of quasilinearity.

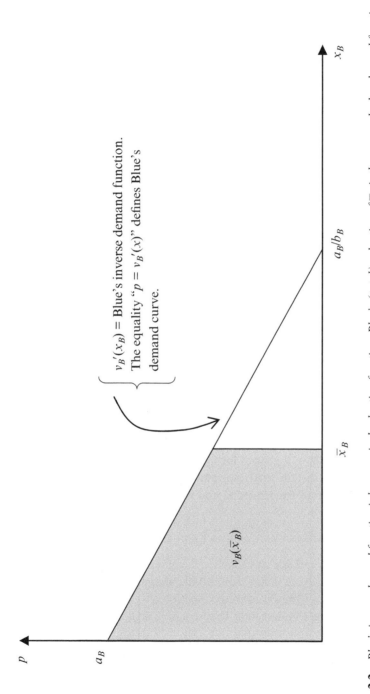

Figure 2.2 *Blue's inverse demand function is her marginal valuation function; Blue's (total) valuation of $\bar{x}_B$ is the area under her demand function from 0 to $\bar{x}_B$*

find $v_B(\bar{x}_B)$, we compute the area under the demand curve from 0 to $\bar{x}_B$ as $v_B(\bar{x}_B) = \int_0^{\bar{x}_B}[a_B - b_B x_B]dx_B = a_B\bar{x}_B - 0.5b_B[\bar{x}_B]^2$. We have then recovered her valuation function $a_B x_B - 0.5b_B[x_B]^2$ from the information provided by her demand function $a_B - b_B x_B$.[7]

2.4.3 Aggregate demand and social valuation

Figure 2.2 indicates that the area under the individual demand of a person equals his or her valuation of a given amount of Good X. Similarly, as long as all consumers face the same price and no consumer is subject to rationing, the area under the aggregate demand curve equals the sum of the valuations of the individual quantities that the consumers demand: see Figure 2.3. Because the area under the aggregate demand curve up to the aggregate amount $\bar{x}$ equals the aggregate or social valuation of $\bar{x}$, the derivative of that area, given by the ordinate of the aggregate demand curve at $\bar{x}$, is the *marginal social valuation* of the aggregate amount $\bar{x}$.

2.4.4 Social surplus as the area between the aggregate demand and marginal social cost curves

We have just seen that the area below the aggregate demand curve is the social valuation of the aggregate quantity, and the aggregate demand curve itself expresses the marginal social valuation of the aggregate quantity. The aggregate supply function in a competitive market has a similar interpretation, but it must be subject to qualification in the presence of fixed costs.

The discussion in Chapter 5 below considers fixed costs, and it is useful to have a general formulation that includes them, even though we will often assume fixed costs away. The general formulation considers costs as the sum of fixed costs, F, and variable costs, $C_v(x)$, as follows:

$$C(x) = \begin{cases} 0 \text{ if } x = 0, \\ F + C_v(x), \text{ if } x > 0, \end{cases}$$

where the variable cost function $C_v(x)$ is increasing and differentiable, with $C_v(0) = 0$. Note that (for $x > 0$) the marginal cost $C'(x)$ equals the derivative $C'_v(x)$ of the variable cost function.

By the Fundamental Theorem of Calculus, for $\bar{x} > 0$,

---

[7] The area can alternatively be computed by elementary geometry as
{*Area of rectangle with base* $[0, \bar{x}_B]$ *and height* $[0, a_B - b_B\bar{x}_B]$}
+ {*Area of triangle with base* $[0,\bar{x}_B]$ *and height* $a_B - [a_B - b_B\bar{x}_B]$}
$= \bar{x}_B[a_B - b_B\bar{x}_B] + 0.5\bar{x}_B[a_B - [a_B - b_B\bar{x}_B]]$
$= \bar{x}_B[a_B - b_B\bar{x}_B] + 0.5\bar{x}_B b_B\bar{x}_B = a_B\bar{x}_B - 0.5b_B[\bar{x}_B]^2$.

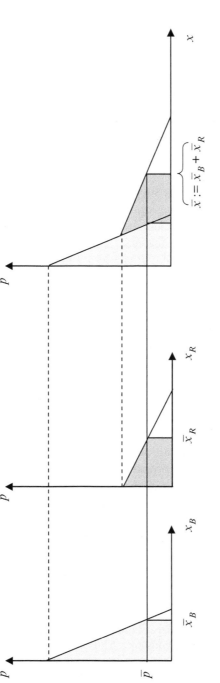

Figure 2.3 *Individual and aggregate valuation as the area under the relevant demand curve*

$$\int_0^{\bar{x}} C'(x)\,\mathrm{d}x = \int_0^{\bar{x}} C_v'(x)\,\mathrm{d}x = C_v(\bar{x}) - C_v(0) = C_v(\bar{x}),$$

i.e.,

$$C(\bar{x}) = \int_0^{\bar{x}} C'(x)\,\mathrm{d}x + F.$$

This formulation will be useful in Chapter 5 and Section 2.4.5 below, but for the remainder of Section 2.4.4 we assume that fixed costs are absent, i.e., $F = 0$. Moreover, let the marginal cost curves of all firms be increasing. Then the marginal cost curve of a firm coincides with its supply curve, and by horizontally adding these supply curves we obtain the aggregate supply curve (as we obtained the aggregate demand curve of Figure 2.3), which in fact coincides with the marginal social cost curve $C'(x)$. Hence in this case, $C(\bar{x})$ is the area under the aggregate supply curve from zero to $\bar{x}$. This is also true when the marginal cost curves are horizontal, in which case the aggregate supply curve is flat, and equilibrium profits are zero.

Because, by definition, *Social surplus := Social valuation – Social cost*, we can visualize the social surplus obtained at the aggregate quantity $\bar{x}$ as the area below the aggregate demand curve (which curve expresses the marginal social valuation) but above the aggregate supply curve (which curve expresses the marginal social cost). The vertical distance between the two curves indicates the marginal social surplus.[8]

The following two figures, which share their demand and supply curves, illustrate. For the aggregate amount $\bar{x}$ in Figure 2.4, $AREA[\overline{A + C}]$ represents the social valuation of $\bar{x}$ units of good X, whereas $AREA[C]$ represents the social cost of producing $\bar{x}$. Hence, $AREA[\overline{A}]$ is the social surplus.

In marginal terms, the ordinate of point θ^H is the marginal social valuation of the amount $\bar{x}$, whereas that of point θ^L is its marginal social cost. We see that, at $\bar{x}$, the marginal social valuation is higher than the marginal social cost, evidencing that the marginal social surplus is positive at $\bar{x}$. Increasing x would therefore increase social surplus.

Figure 2.5 depicts the competitive market equilibrium, where supply equals demand in the amount x^*. Again, $AREA[A^*+C^*]$ represents the social valuation of x^* units of good X, $AREA[C^*]$ represents the social

---

[8] In principle, social surplus depends not only on the aggregate quantity x but also on its distribution among consumers and on the allocation of its production among firms. When we express social surplus in terms of the aggregate quantity x we are implicitly or explicitly assuming "efficient rationing," i.e., that the marginal valuations of all individual consumers coincide, and that the marginal costs of all individual firms also coincide. Of course, this assumption is automatically satisfied at a competitive equilibrium.

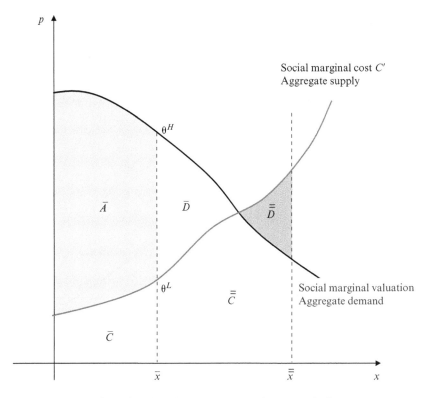

Figure 2.4   *Social surplus when the quantity is too low or too high*

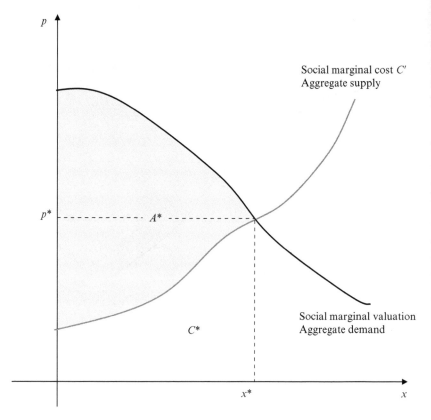

Figure 2.5   *Maximal social surplus at the competitive equilibrium*

cost of producing x^*, and $AREA[A^*]$ is the social surplus. The marginal social valuation at x^* coincides with the marginal social cost: they are both equal to p^*. Consequently, the marginal social surplus is zero.

At the other extreme we have the quantity $\overline{\overline{x}}$ of Figure 2.4: $AREA$ $[\overline{A} + \overline{D} + \overline{C} + \overline{\overline{C}}]$ portrays the social valuation of $\overline{\overline{x}}$ units of good X, whereas $AREA[\overline{C} + \overline{\overline{C}} + \overline{\overline{D}}]$ portrays the social cost of producing $\overline{\overline{x}}$. Hence, $AREA[\overline{A} + \overline{D} - \overline{\overline{D}}]$ is the social surplus reached at $\overline{\overline{x}}$. Note that, at $\overline{\overline{x}}$ the marginal social cost is higher than the marginal social valuation, and therefore the marginal social surplus is negative. Reducing x would increase social surplus.

Figure 2.5 illustrates the First Fundamental Theorem of Welfare Economics. At the point of intersection of supply and demand, the marginal social benefit equals the marginal social cost: surplus is then maximized, at level A^*, in our private-good, no-externality economy.

In Figure 2.4, the level of surplus reached at $\overline{x}$ or at $\overline{\overline{x}}$ is less than the maximum A^*: $AREA[\overline{D}]$ depicts the deadweight loss at $\overline{x}$, and $AREA[\overline{\overline{D}}]$ that of $\overline{\overline{x}}$.

2.4.5   The distribution of social surplus into consumer surplus and profits

We now return to the more general case where there may be fixed costs, i.e., $F \geq 0$. Suppose that a firm (or a group of firms) produces good X, selling x_B units to Blue and x_R units to Red, and collecting T_B units of numeraire from Blue and T_R from Red. Aggregate profits are

$$Profits := T_B + T_R - C(x_B + x_R).$$

We define Blue's (net) consumer surplus as the difference between her valuation or willingness to pay and what she actually pays, i.e.,[9]

$$Blue's\ consumer\ surplus := v_B(x_B) - T_B,$$

and similarly

$$Red's\ consumer\ surplus := v_R(x_R) - T_R.$$

Therefore,

$$[Blue's\ consumer\ surplus] + [Red's\ consumer\ surplus] + [profits]$$

$$= v_B(x_B) - T_B + v_R(x_R) - T_R + T_B + T_R - C(x_B + x_R)$$
$$= v_B(x_B) + v_R(x_R) - C(x_B + x_R),$$

[9] Jules Dupuit (1804–1866) pioneered the analysis of consumer surplus.

which is exactly the expression for social surplus as given in (2.1) above.

The division of social surplus into consumer surplus and profits must be taken into account when evaluating the distributive effects of economic policies.

Let good X be sold at a constant market price $\bar{p}$. Then

$$T_B = \bar{p}\bar{x}_B,$$

$$T_R = \bar{p}\bar{x}_R,$$

and aggregate profits equal $\bar{p}[\bar{x}_B + \bar{x}_R] - C(\bar{x}_B + \bar{x}_R)$. If no consumer is rationed in the market, then $\bar{p} = v'_B(\bar{x}_B) = v'_R(\bar{x}_R)$ (see Section 2.4.2 above), and the consumer surplus of, say, Ms. Blue is given by the area between her demand curve and a horizontal line at the height $\bar{p}$, see Figure 2.6.

We define *Producer surplus = Revenue – Variable cost*. Accordingly,

$$Profits := Revenue - Cost$$

$$= Revenue - Variable\ cost - Fixed\ cost$$

$$= Producer\ surplus - Fixed\ cost.$$

If there are no fixed costs, and the marginal cost curves are not decreasing, then the social marginal cost curve coincides with the competitive supply curve, and profits coincide with producer surplus. Figure 2.5 shows the distribution of surplus between consumer surplus and profits (profits here equal producer surplus) at the competitive equilibrium. Aggregate consumer surplus is the area between the demand curve and the horizontal line at level p^* (up to x^*), whereas aggregate producer surplus is the area between the horizontal line at level p^* and the marginal cost curve. Of course, the sum of these two areas equals total surplus ($AREA[A^*]$).

We need more information about prices (and rationing: recall that we postulate efficient rationing, see footnote 8 above) in order to specify the distribution of surplus at $\bar{x}$ or $\bar{\bar{x}}$ of Figure 2.4. Figure 2.7 reproduces the main elements of Figure 2.4 for $\bar{x}$, but considers two alternative prices. At the high price p^H, consumers satisfy their demands, whereas firms are rationed. Consumer surplus is then $AREA[A_C]$, whereas producer surplus is $AREA[B + A_P]$. But at the low price p^L, consumers are rationed, whereas firms satisfy their competitive supply. Consumer surplus is then $AREA[A_C + B]$, whereas producer surplus is $AREA[A_P]$.

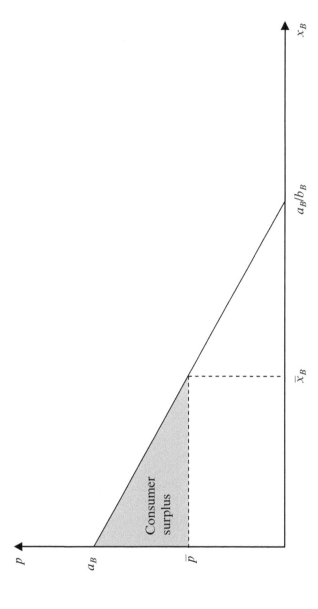

Figure 2.6 *Blue's consumer surplus when the market price is $\bar{p}$ and she is not rationed*

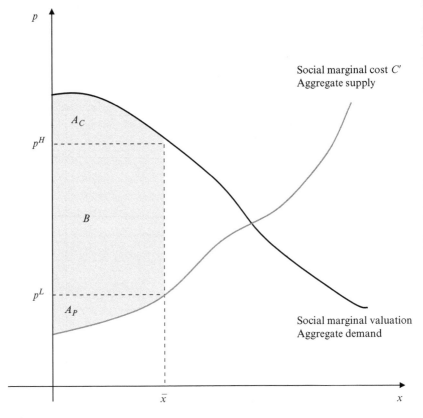

Figure 2.7   *The distribution of social surplus*

Appendix 2A   The First Fundamental Theorem of Welfare Economics in the continuum economy

Our starting point is the economy of Appendix 1A above.

Individual demand. Assume that good X is sold in a market at an impersonal or uniform (same for everybody) price p. Each person then has to decide whether to consume or not, a Yes–No decision. Consider Person n, with initial endowment $\omega(n)$ of numeraire. If she buys, then her utility is $\sqrt{\bar{v}(n)} + \omega(n) - p$. If she does not buy, then her utility is $\sqrt{\omega(n)}$. Therefore, n wishes to buy if the market price p is less than $\bar{v}(n)$, and does not wish to buy if $p > \bar{v}(n)$. The valuation $\bar{v}(n)$ of the good by Person n is then her *reservation price*: see Figure 2A.1.

Aggregate (or market) demand. What is the consumption level $\bar{N}$ demanded at a given price $\bar{p}$? Assume that the valuation function $\bar{v}(n)$ is decreasing when positive-valued, as in Figure 1A.1, and let $\bar{p} > 0$. The consumption level $\bar{N}$ demanded at that price must satisfy:

- Everybody in the interval $(0, \bar{N})$ wishes to buy, i.e., $\bar{p} < \bar{v}(n)$ for $n < \bar{N}$;
- Nobody in the interval $(\bar{N}, N_0]$, wishes to buy, i.e., $\bar{p} > \bar{v}(n)$ for $n > \bar{N}$;
- Hence, $\bar{p} = \bar{v}(n)$ for $n = \bar{N}$: in other words, the person with name $\bar{N}$ is just indifferent between buying or not: she is then called the *marginal consumer* at price $\bar{p}$.

Hence, the market price equals the reservation price of the marginal consumer, and the aggregate, or market, inverse demand curve is given by

$$p = \bar{v}(N).$$

Thus, the aggregate inverse demand curve is precisely the curve of individual valuations of Figure 1A.1 of Appendix 1A above, but with a slightly different interpretation of the axes, see Figure 2A.2. The vertical axis now indicates the market price, whereas the horizontal axis now indicates both the name of a consumer (in particular, the name of the marginal consumer at a given price) and the market level of consumption.

Aggregate valuation. As with a finite number of consumers (see Section 2.4.3 above), the area under the aggregate demand curve gives the aggregate, or social, valuation of a consumption level N, which is now defined as $\int_0^N \bar{v}(n)\,dn$, an expression which already appeared in (1A.2) above. See Figure 2A.2.

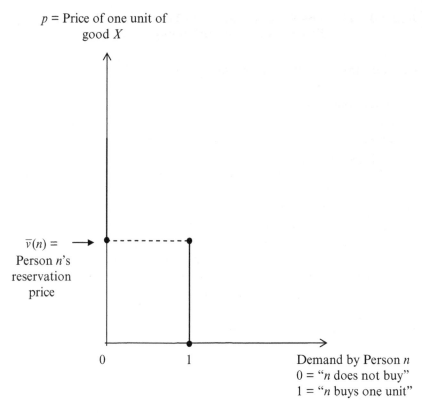

Figure 2A.1   *Demand curve of Person n for a Yes–No good*

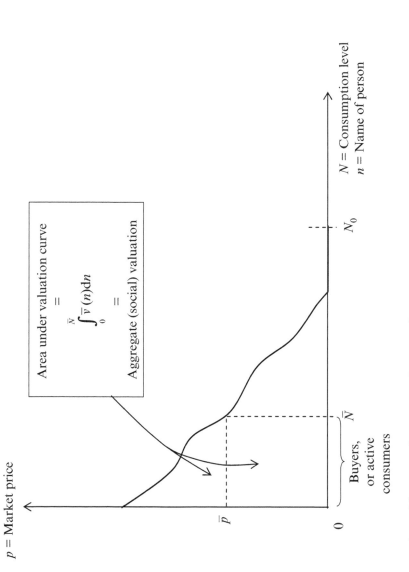

Figure 2A.2 *Aggregate demand function and aggregate valuation in the continuum economy*

First Fundamental Theorem of Welfare Economics. Under competitive conditions, the market supply curve coincides with the marginal cost curve $C'(N)$, and hence the competitive market equilibrium yields the consumption level N^* of Figure 1A.1, resulting in economic efficiency.

Note that Figure 1A.1 looks similar to Figure 2.5, even though the interpretation of the axes is somewhat different. One could also draw a figure similar to Figure 2.4 to represent the deadweight loss when the consumption level is lower or higher than N^*.

Appendix 2B   Potential compensation in quasilinear economies

Recall from Appendix 1D that *a feasible allocation is better than another one in the sense of the compensation principle if and only if it generates a larger social surplus.*

Figure 2.1 can be used to illustrate this fact. Consider a move from A to B: by comparing the utility pairs we can see that Blue gains, and Red loses, from that move. We can also see that the move from A to B increases social surplus, because the utility pair B lies on a higher utility minifrontier than A. Of course, there is no contradiction between the facts that surplus is higher at B, and that Red loses in the move, because the manner in which the numeraire good is distributed among people does not enter in the definition of the surplus, which has as variables only x_B and x_R, and not m_B or m_R.

Allocation B is better than allocation A according to the potential compensation criterion, as can be seen as follows. Let us start at B and fix the xs of allocation B, namely (x_B^*, x_R^*).[10] Let the winner in the move from A to B (Blue) transfer numeraire to the loser. The utility pair will then move northwest along the utility minifrontier going through B. If enough numeraire were transferred in this manner, point C would be reached, better than A for both people. (In other words, C Pareto dominates A.) The existence of a point at C is guaranteed by the fact that the utility minifrontier going through B lies outside (above) the one through A.

The key word here is *potential*. Note that we say that B is better than A in the sense of the potential compensation criterion even if no compensation is in fact paid to the loser. It is the *possibility* of making everyone better off that makes the first allocation better in the sense of potential compensation criterion.

The potential compensation criterion is traditionally justified as follows. Because C can be reached from B just by exchanging numeraire, without creating or destroying any good, one could say that "the size of the pie is the same at B and at C" in a (not uncontroversial) manner of speaking. And C is certainly better than A for both people, thus the "pie" must be larger at C than at A. Hence, the "pie" is also larger at B than at A.

But in actuality the loser will be worse off if the compensation is only potential, in which case he ends up with "a small slice of a larger pie," smaller than his previous "large slice of a smaller pie." The desirability of such a move will depend on the social valuation of the trade-off between the gainer's gain and the loser's loss: see the discussion of social welfare functions in Section 1.5.1 above.

---

[10] The allocation of B is efficient, but this is immaterial: what matters is that the utility minifrontier through B runs northeast of A.

3 Externalities

3.1 Introduction

3.1.1 Concepts

In the case of private goods without externalities, the arguments in the utility function of a person are the amounts of the various goods that she consumes, and not the amounts consumed by other people. But now we consider the possibility that a person's consumption of good X affects the utility of other persons. For instance, Red's utility may depend not only on his consumption x_R of good X and his consumption m_R of numeraire, but also on Blue's consumption x_B of good X, in which case we write Red's utility function as $U_R(x_R, x_B, m_R)$, and we say that Blue's consumption of good X creates an *externality* on Red. The externality could in principle be *positive* (or "good") if Red's utility increased with x_B, and *negative* (or "bad") if it decreased with x_B.

If Blue's consumption generates an externality on Red, but Red's consumption does not generate an externality on Blue, then we say that the externality is *unidirectional*. If the externality runs in both directions, then we say that it is *omnidirectional*, in which case the utility functions would be written $U_B(x_B, x_R, m_B)$ and $U_R(x_R, x_B, m_R)$. More generally, the *generators* and the *recipients* of the externality are distinct groups when the externality is unidirectional, whereas everyone involved is at the same time a generator and a recipient when the externality is omnidirectional.

Here we focus on externalities where both generators and recipients of the externality are consumers, but the externality notion covers also firms. A general definition of externality reads as follows.

Definition. An *externality* is present when the utility function of a consumer, referred to as Consumer i (or the production function of a firm, referred to as Firm j) includes consumption (or production) variables whose values are chosen by other consumers or firms without particular attention to the welfare of Consumer i (or the profits of Firm j).[1]

---

[1] This definition is inspired by William J. Baumol and Wallace E. Oates (1975), *The Theory of Environmental Policy: Externalities, Public Outlays and the Quality of Life*, Englewood Cliffs, NJ: Prentice-Hall.

We then say that Consumer i (or Firm j) is the recipient of the externality. The persons or firms who choose the variables entering Consumer i's utility function (or Firm j's production function) are called the generators of the externality. The connotation is that choices made by generators while pursuing their own self-centered objectives have unintentional side effects on recipients.

Another expression for externalities is *external effects*. An externality involving only firms is called a *production externality*, which if positive can be labeled an *external economy* (or *external economy of scale*), and an *external diseconomy* (or *external diseconomy of scale*) if negative.

Externalities involving large numbers, in particular many recipients, occupy a center stage in public policy. For simplicity of exposition we may often refer to only two economic agents, such as Ms. Blue and Mr. Red, which should be viewed as a metaphor for the realistic cases of many recipients.[2]

3.1.2   Examples of externalities

Environmental externalities
The emission of pollutants often affects the quality of the environment. Nicholas Stern (2008) writes, "Greenhouse gas (GHG) emissions are externalities and represent the biggest market failure that the world has seen."[3] These affect the global environment, and involve a degree of uni-directionality since emissions today will affect the welfare of generations not yet born.

The extinction of species due to human activity presents another example of global environmental externality, and so does the destruction of the stratospheric ozone layer from discharges of chlorofluorocarbons. On the other hand, some environmental externalities are regional or local. Acid precipitation in the northeastern United States and some Canadian provinces provides an example of regional externality: SO_2, sulfur oxides, nitrogen oxides and other harmful acidic components are generated by automobile, power plants and coal burning and are then deposited on the ground by rain, snow and fog. The unhealthy levels of air pollution in the Los Angeles basin due to emissions by automobile and power plants provide an example of local environmental externality.

---

[2] The approach to externalities pioneered by Ronald Coase focuses, on the contrary, on externalities involving one generator and one recipient, see Section 3.6 and Appendix 3B below. Coase (born 2010) was awarded the 1991 Nobel Prize in Economic Sciences.

[3] N. Stern (2008), "The economics of climate change," *American Economic Review: Papers and Proceedings*, 98(2), 1–37.

The commons

This type of externality is present when many users exploit and deplete a natural resource, such as a fishery, pastureland, oilfield, aquifer or forest. This is a negative externality, usually omnidirectional and involving production. But it could also be unidirectional, e.g., the use of a river for irrigation, where the upstream irrigators are generators, but not recipients, of the externality.

Congestion

Congested transportation systems provide examples of negative, omnidirectional externalities: any additional user of a congested facility decreases the value of the facility to every other user.

We consider positive externalities next.

Vaccination

By vaccinating your child you generate a positive externality on all your child's classmates, who will now face a lower probability of contagion. More generally, improvements in individual wellness often generate positive externalities by contributing to public health.

Education

The investment in education benefits not only the person who undertakes it but also many people who will interact with the person. Public sector expenditures in education and health have a double motivation. From the efficiency viewpoint, they aim at attenuating the market failures due to the accompanying externalities, but at the same time they address concerns of equality of opportunity.

Network externalities

The value of an uncongested network, such as telephone or e-mail, to its users often increases with the number of users. Hence, joining the network may well enhance its value to all users.

Agglomeration externalities

The historical development of cities illustrates location externalities: when an economic agent locates close to other agents, the cost of interaction decreases. This effect is the positive counterpart to congestion externalities.

Endogenous growth

Firms create knowledge by learning-by-doing and by intentional investment in R&D. Some of this knowledge may spill over to other firms in the same sector or geographical area (as, e.g., in Silicon Valley). The patent system may limit these spillovers, but at the same time it may foster them by making the discoveries public knowledge. These externalities, a form of external economies of scale, underpin modern economic growth theory.

3.1.3   The externality market failure

Because the externality occurs as a by-product of activities that pursue other interests, the decision makers may fail to take into account external effects when deciding on the level of the activity. The outcome will then be that of a Cournot–Nash equilibrium, typically inefficient (see Appendix 1B above). Relative to the efficient level, a Cournot–Nash equilibrium will entail too little of the externality causing activity for positive externalities, and too much when the externality is negative. Recall that the First Fundamental Theorem of Welfare Economics does not apply when externalities are present.

Sometimes policy intervention is not needed because the participants manage to implement an efficient level of the externality through co-operation or agreement. Consider a unidirectional externality with a single generator and a single recipient, who may reach a private agreement on the level of the externality involving some money transfer between the two: the tradition that follows Coase focuses in these cases.

Or perhaps the users of a common pool resource cooperate in devising and enforcing efficient rules of access and exploitation, as emphasized in the literature pioneered by Elinor Ostrom.[4] In fact, there is by now an extensive literature on the communal management of common pool resources (catalogued by the *Digital Library of the Commons*, Indiana University http://dlc.dlib.indiana.edu) which documents many instances of efficient utilization of the resource. Yet inefficient overuse is also a frequent occurrence.

Sections 3.2 to 3.5 below study externality situations lacking agreements or communal institutions and the appropriate policy measures. Bilateral agreements are discussed in Section 3.6 and Appendix 3B below.

3.2   Unidirectional negative externalities

3.2.1   A two-person model

Two people, Blue and Red. Blue's consumption of good X generates a negative externality on Red, while Red's consumption does not generate

---

[4] E. Ostrom (1990), *Governing the Commons: The Evolution of Institutions for Collective Action*, Cambridge: Cambridge University Press. Ostrom (born 1933) was awarded the 2009 Nobel Prize in Economic Sciences.

any externality. Think of Blue as being located upstream of Red on a river, with Blue's consumption of good X emitting water pollutants that negatively affect the utility of Red. Choose units such that the amount of pollutants, Z, equals Blue's consumption x_B of Good X. The utility functions are

$$U_B(x_B, m_B) = \sqrt{v_B(x_B)} + m_B, \; v_B(0) = 0,$$

$$U_R(x_R, Z, m_R) = \sqrt{v_R(x_R) - \gamma(Z)} + m_R,$$
$$\text{where } Z = x_B, \, v_B(0) = 0, \gamma(0) = 0,$$

see Figure 3.1: as in previous chapters, $v_B(x_B)$ (resp. $v_R(x_R)$) is Blue's (resp. Red's) valuation of her (resp. his) own consumption of good X. The quantity Z, here equal to x_B, is the level of the *externality variable*, or the *externality causing activity*, whereas $\gamma(Z)$ is the *external damage*, or *external cost*, function. In many of the examples we take $\gamma(Z)$ to be a linear function, namely $\gamma(Z) = gZ$. The resource cost of producing good X is linear, namely $C(x_B + x_R) = c[x_B + x_R]$, with constant marginal cost c. Blue (resp. Red) initially owns ω_B (resp. ω_R) units of numeraire.

3.2.2   Surplus maximization

Social surplus is, as in Chapter 1 above, the aggregate valuation or benefit minus the cost. Because of the externality, Red's benefit depends now on both his consumption x_R and Blue's consumption x_B and associated emissions. Recalling that $Z = x_B$, we write the social surplus function as

$$S(x_B, x_R): = v_B(x_B) + v_R(x_R) - c[x_B + x_R] - \gamma(x_B). \tag{3.1}$$

The maximization of (3.1) requires (partially) differentiating this expression first with respect to x_B and then to x_R. The derivative with respect to x_B is $v_B'(x_B) - c - \gamma'(x_B)$. If this expression is negative or zero for $x_B = 0$, i.e., $v_B'(0) \le c + \gamma'(0)$, then efficiency requires that $x_B = 0$.[5] We will assume in what follows that $v_B'(0) > c + \gamma'(0)$ so that efficiency requires $x_B > 0$. A marginal condition for efficiency is obtained by setting the just computed partial derivative equal to zero. When $v_B(x_B) = a_B x_B - 0.5 b_B[x_B]^2$ and $\gamma(x_B) = g x_B$, we solve the equation $a_B - b_B x_B - c - g = 0$, yielding

---

[5] The production or consumption of good X by Blue is then banned, as may happen in some hazardous or unhealthy products. For instance, the Montreal Protocol of 1987 banned the production of chlorofluorocarbons.

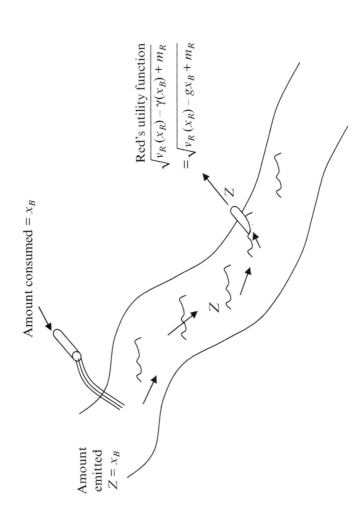

Figure 3.1 *Unidirectional, negative externality*

$$a_B - b_B x_B = c + g,$$

which can be read as:

$$\text{Marginal social benefit} = \text{Marginal social cost}, \tag{3.2}$$

where the marginal social cost has two components: the marginal resource or production cost c, and the marginal external damage g.[6] The solution to this equation is

$$x_B^* = \frac{a_B - c - g}{b_B}. \tag{3.3}$$

See Figure 3.2.

Because Red does not generate any externality, the marginal condition obtained by differentiating (3.1) with respect to x_R coincides with that of the case of no externalities studied in Chapter 2, i.e., $v_R'(x_R) - c = 0$. For $v_R(x_R) = a_R x_R - 0.5 b_R [x_R]^2$, it yields $a_R - b_R x_R = c$. The solution to this equation is, as in Chapter 2 above,

$$x_R^* = \frac{a_R - c}{b_R}. \tag{3.4}$$

3.2.3   Free-market equilibrium

The *free-market* allocation is the one obtained at the general competitive equilibrium: because the conditions of the First Fundamental Theorem of Welfare Economics are not satisfied in the presence of externalities, we should not expect the free-market allocation to be efficient. Blue decides on the quantity, to be denoted $\tilde{x}_B$, which she buys in the market at the competitive equilibrium price $p = c$ (or that Blue can produce at marginal cost c). Thus, Blue maximizes $\sqrt{v_B(x_B)} + \omega_B - c x_B$. For $v_B(x_B) = a_B x_B - 0.5 b_B [x_B]^2$, the first-order condition is

$$a_B - b_B x_B = c, \tag{3.5}$$

which can be interpreted as

$$\text{Marginal internal benefit} = \text{Marginal internal cost}, \tag{3.6}$$

---

[6] Of course, there is no externality when $g = 0$, in which case the equation reduces to the equality between marginal valuation and marginal cost seen in Chapter 2 above for the case of a private good not subject to externalities.

Marginal internal benefit
Marginal internal cost
Marginal external cost
Marginal social cost

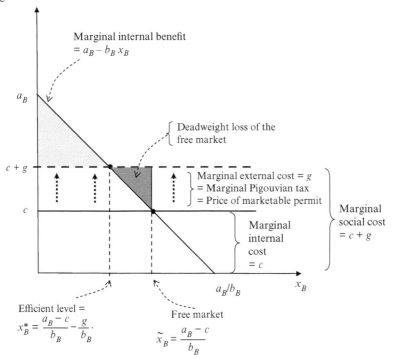

Figure 3.2   *Efficiency and the free market in a negative unidirectional externality*

where, following Pigou, we use the term *internal* to refer to the costs or benefits that the decision maker takes into consideration.[7] Comparing with (3.2) above, we observe that, for Blue's consumption,

Marginal social benefit = Marginal internal benefit $= a_B - b_B x_B,$

whereas the marginal external cost creates a gap between the marginal social cost and the marginal internal cost, i.e.,

Marginal social cost = Marginal internal cost

$+$ *Marginal external cost* $= c + g,$

Equation (3.5) defines the free-market equilibrium consumption of good X by Blue as

$$\widetilde{x}_B = \frac{a_B - c}{b_B}, \tag{3.7}$$

see Figure 3.2.

As for Red, at the free-market allocation he takes Blue's consumption x_B as given, and maximizes $\sqrt{v_R(x_R)} + \omega_R - c x_R - \gamma(x_B)$. For $v_R(x_R) = a_R x_R - 0.5 b_R [x_R]^2$, the first order condition is $a_R - b_R x_R = c$. Red's consumption does not generate any externality, and hence there is no difference between the internal and social marginal costs of his consumption, and Red's free-market allocation coincides with (3.4), i.e.,

$$\widetilde{x}_R = x_R^* = \frac{a_R - c}{b_R}.$$

Because $g > 0$ (the externality is negative), we see from (3.3) and (3.7) that $x_B^* < \widetilde{x}_B$, i.e., there is too much externality-causing activity at the free-market allocation: the dark triangle in Figure 3.2 depicts its deadweight loss. Of course, the inequality would be reversed were the externality positive, see Section 3.4 below.

3.2.4 Policy instruments for negative externalities

Public policy targeted at the inefficiency of the free-market solution under negative externalities can take any of the three following forms.

1.   *Nontransferable quotas* or *standards*. Generators are forbidden to engage in the externality-causing activity in excess of its efficient level.

---

[7] Arthur Cecil Pigou (1877–1959) pioneered the study of externalities in his 1920 book *The Economics of Welfare* (London: Macmillan).

2. *Pigouvian taxes.* Generators are free to decide on the level of the externality-causing activity, but must pay a tax, called a Pigouvian tax (after Pigou), with marginal tax rate equal to the marginal external damage at the efficient allocation.
3. *Cap-and-trade* schemes (or *transferable permits*, or *marketable permits*). The public sector issues a total number of permits equal to the total level of the externality-causing activity at the efficient allocation, and these permits can then be freely traded.

3.2.5 Pigouvian tax

We continue with the Blue and Red model of Sections 3.2.1–3.2.3 above. Define the Pigouvian marginal tax rate

$$t^* = g. \tag{3.8}$$

Under a (linear) Pigouvian tax, Blue has to pay the amount $t^* x_B$ for the right to emit the amount x_B. Intuitively, the Pigouvian marginal tax rate fills the gap between the marginal *social* cost of Blue's consumption ($c + g$, as given by (3.2)) and its marginal *internal* cost (just c, as in (3.6)). In other words, the Pigouvian marginal tax rate equals the marginal damage imposed on others (here, on Red), or the *marginal external cost*.

An important observation: Pigouvian taxes should be understood as instruments for giving the decision makers the correct marginal incentives, not as a way of compensating the recipients of a negative externality, see Sections 3.6.5 and 3B.3 below.[8]

3.2.6 Cap and trade

The public sector issues x_B^* marketable permits. These permits can be given away free of charge to the members of society or auctioned off, so that the public sector collects some revenue. The permits can then be traded in what is often called the *secondary* market for permits. (The auction is the primary market when permits are auctioned off.)

Let the public sector issue a fixed amount $Z^* = x_B^*$ of permits, as given by (3.3) above. At what price r^* of a permit will "the market" demand exactly Z^* permits? Here only Blue is interested in buying. Assuming that Blue is a price taker, her demand for permits can be computed as follows. If the market price of a permit is r units of numeraire, and Blue already owns $\bar{x}_B > 0$ permits, then she has to choose the amount x_B of emissions that maximizes

---

[8] For instance, Blue could receive a subsidy not to emit in the amount $H - t^* x_B$, $H > 0$, decreasing in x_B. Formally, this is a nonlinear (actually, affine) tax scheme.

$$\sqrt{a_B x_B - 0.5 b_B [x_B]^2 + \omega_B - c x_B - r[x_B - \overline{x}_B]},$$

with first-order condition

$$a_B - b_B x_B - c - r = 0, \qquad (3.9)$$

i.e., Blue's *gross* demand for permits as a function of r is

$$x_B = \frac{a_B - c - r}{b_B}. \qquad (3.10)$$

We subtract $\overline{x}_B$ from (3.10) to obtain Blue's *net* demand for permits.

Expression (3.9) gives Blue's demand-for-permits curve: it can be drawn by translating downwards the marginal internal benefit curve of Figure 3.2 by the amount c, and writing the price r of a permit on the vertical axis: see Figure 3.3.

The equilibrium price r^* of the permits must satisfy the condition

Aggregate gross demand of permits = Total supply of permits,

where the total supply of permits is given by (3.3) above as $Z^* = x_B^* :=$ $[a_B - c - g]/b_B$. Solving for r the equation $[a_B - c - r]/b_B = [a_B - c - g]/b_B$ we obtain $r^* = g$, see Figure 3.3. In words, the equilibrium price r^* of a permit equals the Pigouvian marginal tax rate t^*. It follows that a Pigouvian tax and a cap-and-trade system give externality-generating agents the same marginal incentives to emit at the efficient level by setting an "externality marginal price" of $t^* = r^* = g$. Moreover, the total revenue obtained from the linear Pigouvian tax, $t^* x_B^*$, equals the equilibrium market value of the permits issued, which would also coincide with the revenue obtained from a perfectly competitive auction of those permits.

3.2.7 Distributional flexibility

Point $\tilde{U}$ in the utility possibility set of Figure 3.4 depicts the utility levels reached at the free-market allocation, with coordinates $\tilde{U}_B = \sqrt{a_B \tilde{x}_B - 0.5 b_B [\tilde{x}_B]^2 + \omega_B - c \tilde{x}_B}$ and $\tilde{U}_R \equiv$ $\sqrt{a_R x_R^* - 0.5 b_R [x_R^*]^2 - g \tilde{x}_B + \omega_R - c x_R^*}$. (Recall that $\tilde{x}_R = x_R^*$.) Because the free-market allocation is inefficient, $\tilde{U}$ does not lie on the utility possibilities frontier.[9]

Under nontransferable quotas, no numeraire changes hands among

---

[9] Recall that the utility possibilities frontier is a circle of radius $\sqrt{S^* + \omega}$, where S^* is the maximal surplus.

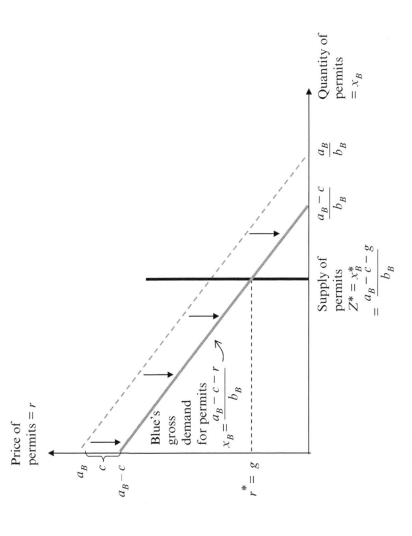

Figure 3.3 *Equilibrium in the market for permits*

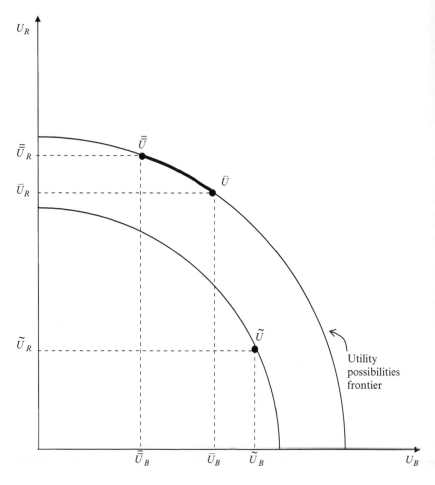

Figure 3.4 *Utility outcomes in the unidirectional externality*

consumers, or between consumers and the public sector. The utility levels achieved at an efficient nontransferable quota are:

$$\overline{U}_B := \sqrt{a_B x_B^* - 0.5 b_B [x_B^*]^2} + \omega_B - c x_B^*,$$

and

$$\overline{U}_R := \sqrt{a_R x_R^* - 0.5 b_R [x_R^*]^2} - g x_B^* + \omega_R - c x_R^*,$$

see point $\overline{U}$ in the utility possibilities frontier of Figure 3.4. That would also be the utility pair reached under cap and trade if the public sector gave all permits to Blue.

But if the public sector initially gives all the permits to Red, who then sells them to Blue at the equilibrium permit price, then Blue ends up paying Red the amount $r^* x_B^*$, and the utility levels reached are:

$$\overline{\overline{U}}_B := \sqrt{a_B x_B^* - 0.5 b_B [x_B^*]^2} + \omega_B - c x_B^* - r^* x_B^*,$$

and

$$\overline{\overline{U}}_R := \sqrt{a_R x_R^* - 0.5 b_R [x_R^*]^2} - g x_B^* + \omega_R - c x_R^* + r^* x_B^*,$$

see point $\overline{\overline{U}}$. By apportioning the amount x_B^* of permits between Blue and Red any point in the arc $[\overline{U}, \overline{\overline{U}}]$ can be reached.

With a (linear) Pigouvian tax, the government collects the amount $t^* x_B^*$ of tax revenue, equal to the value $r^* x_B^*$ of the permits in a cap-and-trade system. Appropriate lumpsum transfers of the tax revenue to consumers can also lead to any point in the arc $[\overline{U}, \overline{\overline{U}}]$. Accordingly, under the simplifying assumptions of this section, which include complete information and certainty, Pigouvian taxation and cap-and-trade systems are equivalent in terms of inducing efficiency and, contrary to nontransferable quotas, they both provide flexible instruments to address equity concerns.[10,11]

---

[10] Utility pairs on the utility possibilities frontier southeast of $\overline{U}$, in particular northwest of $\tilde{U}$, may in principle be reached under an affine tax schedule $- H + t^* x_B$, for $H > 0$ (a subsidy to Blue) and large enough in absolute value.

[11] We ignore possible losses due to the distribution mechanism, see the reference to Okun's leaky buckets in Chapter 1 above. We also ignore possible gains resulting from replacing distortionary taxation, such as taxes on labor income, by the Pigouvian taxation of externalities (the so-called *double dividend of Pigouvian taxation*).

3.2.8   More than one generator

Cap-and-trade schemes, as well as Pigouvian taxes, have an important additional advantage over nontransferable quotas when several economic agents generate the negative externality, as is by and large the case. Postulate three consumers, Blue, Gray and Red: both Blue and Gray generate a unidirectional externality on Red. The utilities and endowments are as follows.

- Blue's utility (as in the previous section):

$$\sqrt{v_B(x_B)} + m_B = \sqrt{a_B x_B - 0.5 b_B [x_B]^2} + m_B;$$

- Gray's utility: $\sqrt{v_G(x_G)} + m_G = \sqrt{a_G x_G - 0.5 b_G [x_G]^2} + m_G;$
- Red's utility: $\sqrt{v_R(x_R)} + m_R - \gamma(Z)$
$= \sqrt{a_R x_R - 0.5 b_R [x_R]^2} + m_R - gZ$, where $Z = x_B + x_G$.

Following the steps in the previous sections, surplus maximization requires: $x_B^* = [a_B - c - g]/b_B$, $x_G^* = [a_G - c - g]/b_G$, $x_R^* = [a_R - c]/b_R$, with the efficient level of emissions $Z^* = x_B^* + x_G^* = [a_B - c - g]/b_B + [a_G - c - g]/b_G$. How do the three policy approaches perform as instruments for efficiency?

1. *Nontransferable quotas.* In order to achieve efficiency, *the quotas must be personalized*, i.e., x_B^* for Blue and x_G^* for Gray. If the policy maker only has aggregate information, knowing the sum Z^* but not the distribution of Z^* between x_B^* and x_G^*, then it cannot implement personalized quotas. Uniform quotas, say at $0.5 Z^*$ each for Blue and Gray, will induce inefficiency. Figure 3.5 illustrates: the deadweight loss is the sum of the shaded triangles.
2. *Pigouvian taxes.* A uniform tax rate, at $t^* = g$, leads to efficiency.
3. *Cap and trade.* As seen in Section 3.2.4 above, the public sector issues the number of permits corresponding to the sum of the surplus-maximizing emissions, here equal to $Z^* = x_B^* + x_G^*$.

Let the public sector give, free of charge, the permit amounts $\bar{x}_B$, $\bar{x}_G$ and $\bar{x}_R$ to Blue, Gray and Red, respectively, with $\bar{x}_B + \bar{x}_G + \bar{x}_R = Z^*$. The gross demand for permits by Blue as a function of the market price r of a permit is given by (3.9) above. That of Gray is similarly computed as $[a_G - c - r]/b_G$. Hence, the equality of supply and demand requires $[a_B - c - r]/b_B + [a_G - c - r]/b_G = Z^* := [a_B - c - g]/b_B + [a_G - c - g]/b_G$, an equation that is obviously satisfied at $r^* = g$, leading to efficiency. (It can be checked that this solution is unique.)

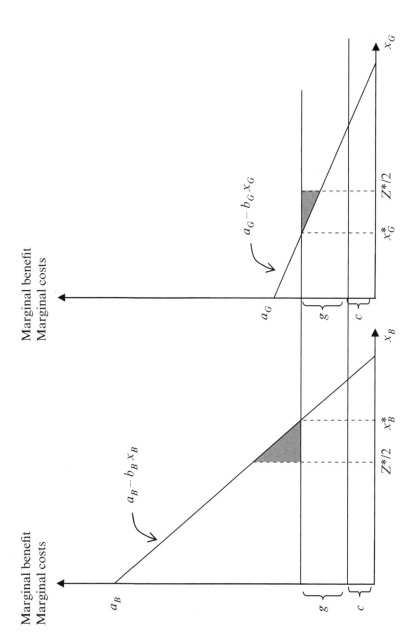

Figure 3.5 *The deadweight loss of uniform quotas*

3.2.9   Comparison of policies

Both nontransferable quotas and cap and trade are *quantity* mechanisms in the sense that they fix the total amount of the externality-causing activity, whereas a Pigouvian tax regulates by *price*: we will see in Section 6.2 of Chapter 6 below that this makes a difference when there is uncertainty in the magnitude of the costs or benefits. But cap and trade gives price incentives similar to a tax to an individual agent, who can freely decide on the level of the externality-causing activity as long as she buys enough permits at the going price.

All three policies may in principle bring about the surplus-maximizing solution. But, as just argued, nontransferable quotas have to be personalized, which requires the policy maker to have detailed information about individual characteristics. Pigouvian taxes, or cap and trade, on the contrary, require only aggregate information. Also as noted, nontransferable quotas are ill-suited to address equity considerations, while Pigouvian taxes, or cap and trade, can distribute the revenue generated by taxes or auctions, or apportion the total number of marketable permits.

3.3   Omnidirectional externalities: North and South

3.3.1   The model

Assume for simplicity that the world is comprised of two countries or regions, North and South, with a large number of consumers in each: there are I_N consumers in North, numbered 1 to I_N, and I_S consumers in South, numbered $I_N + 1$ to $I_N + I_S$. All consumers engage in an externality-causing activity. The externality is omnidirectional, within countries and across them, but it can in principle be positive or negative. An example of a negative externality is the burning of fossil fuels that create GHG (greenhouse gases) which in turn induce the negative effects of global warming. The burning of fossil fuels is useful for the production of energy, transportation,. . ., but the presence of GHG in the stratosphere changes global climate.

Formally, the consumption of good X, carbon in the example, creates the externality. The utility of Consumer i depends on the direct benefits that she derives from her use of the amount x_i of carbon, on the aggregate quantity $Z = \Sigma_{j=1}^{I_N + I_S} x_j$ of GHG in the atmosphere, and, as usual, on the amount m_i of numeraire that she ends up with.[12]

---

[12] This assumes a linear relationship between use of fossil fuels and GHG emissions, as well as a linear relation between GHG emissions and the stock Z of GHG in the atmosphere. In addition, we choose to measure consumption of

All consumers in North have the same utility function: in particular, the utility function for Consumer i in North ($i = 1, \ldots, I_N$) is

$$U_N(x_i, Z, m_i) = \sqrt{v_N(x_i)} - \gamma_N(Z) + m_i, \tag{3.10}$$

where, as usual, x_i (resp. m_i) is her consumption of good X (resp. numeraire), and where $v_N(0) = \gamma_N(0) = 0$. We take $\gamma_N(Z)$ to be an increasing function, indicating that the externality is negative. For most of the analysis, we take the valuation function to be quadratic, i.e., $v_N(x_i) = a_N x_i - 0.5 b_N [x_i]^2$, the damage function to be linear, i.e., $\gamma_N(Z) = g_N Z$, and the individual endowment of numeraire, ω_N, to be identical for any consumer in North. We also assume that the unit cost of production of good X is constant, denoted c and equal to the international competitive market price.

For consumer h in South ($h = I_{N+1}, \ldots, I_N + I_S$) we write: $U_S(x_h, Z, m_h) = \sqrt{v_S(x_h)} - \gamma_S(Z) + m_h$, with $v_S(x_h) = a_S x_h - 0.5 b_S [x_h]^2$ and $\gamma_S(Z) = g_S Z$ as typical functional forms, and with individual endowment of numeraire ω_S.

3.3.2   Free-market allocation

We define the free-market allocation by the competitive equilibrium, both national and international, in the absence of externality policies, domestic or international. (This roughly corresponds to what in the climate change literature is called BAU, or business as usual.) Accordingly, Consumer i of North chooses x_i in order to maximize (3.10), with first order condition $v_N'(x_i) - \gamma_N'(Z) - c = 0$, or if the valuation function is quadratic and the damage function linear, $a_N - b_N x_i - c - g_N = 0$. This equation is the same for all consumers in North, and yields North's free-market individual consumption level $\tilde{x}_N = [a_N - c - g_N]/b_N$, see Figure 3.6. Similarly, South's free-market individual consumption level is $\tilde{x}_S = [a_S - c - g_S]/b_S$.

In this model with many people, we should think of the marginal individual damage g_N as being close to zero.

3.3.3   The nationalistic solution

Because all people in North have the same valuation and damage functions, they will be consuming the same amount of good X, to be denoted x_N, at any interesting allocation: we can view x_N as the consumption of the representative individual in North, with total consumption of good X in North equal to $I_N x_N$. We define North's *nationalistic solution* as

fuel, GHG emissions and the stock of GHG in the atmosphere in the same units, such as gigatons of carbon (GtC).

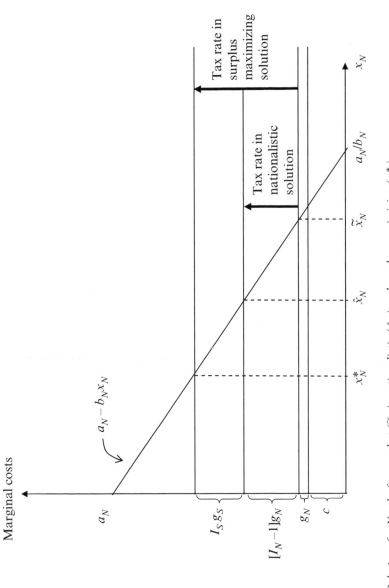

Figure 3.6 *Solutions for North: free market ($\tilde{x}_N$), nationalistic ($\hat{x}_N$) and surplus-maximizing (x_N^*)*

follows: the government of North takes the emissions Z_S from South as given, and chooses x_N in order to maximize the social surplus in North, given by

$$I_N[v_N(x_N) - cx_N - \gamma_N(I_N x_N + Z_S)].$$

The first order condition is (using the chain rule):

$$v'_N(x_N) - c - I_N \gamma'_N(I_N x_N + Z_S) = 0.$$

In the case of quadratic valuation and linear external damage, this equation becomes $a_N - b_N x_N - c - I_N g_N = 0$, with solution $\hat{x}_N = [a_N - c - I_N g_N]/b_N$, see Figure 3.6. Now the product of the small number g_N and the large number I_N can be of significant magnitude.

Similarly, x_S denotes the consumption of an individual in South, with total consumption of good X in South equal to $I_S x_S$. The nationalistic individual consumption in South is then $\hat{x}_S = [a_S - c - I_S g_S]/b_S$.

The nationalistic solution can be implemented via quotas, taxes or cap and trade. The tax rate in the North, equal to the equilibrium price of permits, would equal the marginal external effect on consumers of North $[I_N - 1]g_N$ (see Figure 3.6), very close to $I_N g_N$.

Note that if the nationalistic solution is implemented via quotas, or if the tax revenues or the marketable permits are distributed uniformly, then the representative consumers of North and South are better off than at their free-market allocation. Figure 3.7 (in the spirit of Figure 3.4) illustrates the utility pairs reached at the free-market allocations, namely $\tilde{U}$, and those of the nationalistic solutions, namely $\hat{U}$.[13]

3.3.4 Social (world) surplus

Because $Z = I_S x_S + I_N x_N$, social (i.e., world) surplus can be written as the function of x_S and x_N given by:

$$S(x_S, x_N) := I_S[v_S(x_S) - cx_S - \gamma_S(I_S x_S + I_N x_N)]$$

$$+ I_N[v_N(x_N) - cx_N - \gamma_N(I_S x_S + I_N x_N)],$$

Hence, surplus maximization requires (again using the chain rule):

---

[13] The approach in Section 2.2 of Chapter 2 above shows that a utility minifrontier is here an ellipse defined by the equation $I_S[U_S]^2 + I_N[U_N]^2 = S(x_S, x_N) + \omega$, where ω is the world endowment of numeraire.

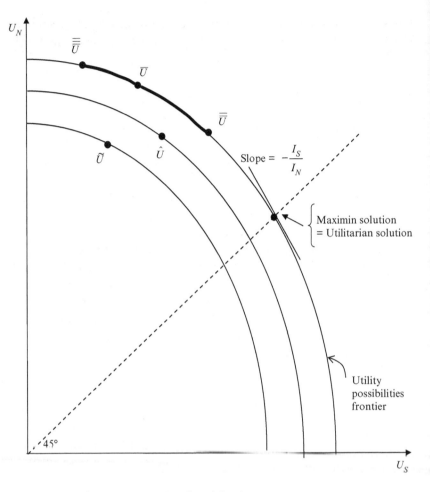

Figure 3.7   *Utility outcomes in North and South*

$$I_S[v'_S(x_S) - c - \gamma'_S(I_S x_S + I_N x_N)I_S] - I_N \gamma'_N(I_S x_S + I_N x_N)I_S = 0,$$

and

$$I_N[v'_N(x_N) - c - \gamma'_N(I_S x_S + I_N x_N)I_N] - I_S \gamma'_S(I_S x_S + I_N x_N)I_N = 0.$$

For quadratic valuations and linear damages, the first equation becomes $I_S[a_S - b_S x_S - c - g_S I_S] - g_N I_N I_S = 0$, with solution

$$x^*_S = \frac{a_S - c - g_S}{b_S} - \frac{g_S[I_S - 1] + g_N I_N}{b_S}.$$

Similarly, for North,

$$x^*_N = \frac{a_N - c - g_N}{b_N} - \frac{g_N[I_N - 1] + g_S I_S}{b_N}.$$

3.3.5 Surplus maximization and international fairness

As before, we can consider nontransferable quotas, Pigouvian taxes or cap-and-trade schemes. The Pigouvian tax rate in the North would be $[I_N - 1]g_N + I_S g_S$, very close to $t^* \equiv I_N g_N + I_S g_S$, and that in the South $[I_S - 1]g_S + I_N g_N \approx t^*$. In a cap-and-trade system, the world equilibrium price of permits would also be very close to t^*. As discussed in Section 3.2.7 above, Pigouvian taxes and cap-and-trade systems may address fairness or equity concerns.

It may well occur that at a surplus-maximizing solution with nontransferable quotas, one of the countries is worse off than at its nationalistic solution, as illustrated by point $\overline{U}$ in Figure 3.7. But by allocating all permits to South (or by transferring to South all tax revenue), the utility of the representative South consumer could possibly be made better off than at the nationalistic solution, as illustrated by point $\overline{\overline{U}}$ in Figure 3.7. At the other extreme, if all permits were allocated to North, then a point such as $\overline{\overline{\overline{U}}}$ in Figure 3.7 would be reached.

Figure 3.7 also illustrates the maximization of the social welfare functions studied in Chapter 1 above. The Rawlsian maximin equates the utilities of the representative consumers in North and South. Utilitarianism, which maximizes $I_N U_N + I_S U_S$, also yields equal utilities here, as it did in Section 1.8.4 above.

3.4 Positive externalities

By letting the external "damage" function $\gamma(Z)$ be *decreasing*, the models of the previous sections can be adapted to a positive externality. Consider, for instance, the simple Blue–Red model of Section 3.2.1 above, and let $g < 0$. Expressions (3.3) and (3.7) remain valid, but of course free markets would now entail an inefficiently low level of the externality-causing activity, see Figure 3.8.

In order to induce the efficient level, quotas or permits will no longer be applicable. A quantity constraint would now take the form of a compulsory *minimal* level of x_B^* for the externality-causing activity. This will be unrealistic in many contexts, but not always: think of compulsory education, or compulsory removal of fire hazards in private housing.[14]

A Pigouvian scheme will now require a *negative* marginal tax rate, i.e., a marginal *subsidy*, at the rate $[-g] > 0$, which is the marginal external benefit that Blue's consumption generates on Red, see Figure 3.8.

Appendix 3A below analyses an interesting instance of ominidirectional, positive externalities, namely network externalities.

3.5 Emission abatement

3.5.1 The upstream–downstream model with abatement

We go back to the Blue–Red negative externality model of Section 3.2 above, where Blue, located upstream, emits a pollutant that affects Red's welfare. Parties involved in a negative externality often have access to techniques that abate or mitigate the external effect. For instance, Blue could perhaps install a filter for its emissions (*abatement*), or perhaps the filter could be installed downstream by Red (*mitigation*). Here we limit ourselves to the situation where Blue, the emitter, has access to an emission-abatement technology, while either the recipient cannot mitigate the effects of the externality, or his mitigating costs are already incorporated in the external damage function.

This new assumption on what is physically possible requires the modification of the social surplus function. First, abatement costs must be introduced in the definition of social surplus. Second, under abatement, Blue's consumption x_B of good X may differ from the amount Z of emissions reaching Red, and both variables must be considered (in addition to x_R) when defining social surplus.

We continue to measure emissions and the consumption of good X in the same units, and accordingly, we also measure the amount abated, denoted α, as the difference between x_B and Z, i.e.,

---

[14] Many policies, such as compulsory education, that either require minimum levels of an activity or subsidize it aim at both efficiency and equity targets.

Marginal internal benefit
Marginal internal cost
Marginal Pigouvian subsidy

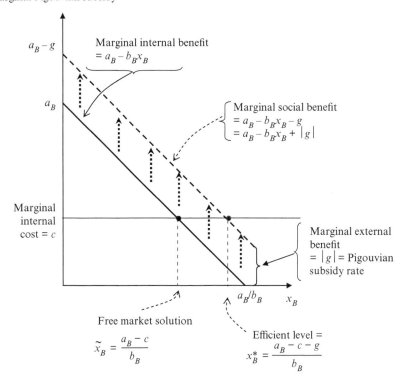

Figure 3.8   *A positive unidirectional externality (g < 0)*

$$\alpha = x_B - Z,$$

or equivalently

$$Z = x_B - \alpha, \tag{3.11}$$

where we suppose that $x_B \geq Z \geq 0$.

Think of the abatement technology as a filter, portrayed by the circle in Figure 3.9, which removes α units of potential emissions, so that the amount of emissions actually reaching the river, and Red, is $Z = x_B - \alpha$.[15] The external damage imposed on Red is now $\gamma(Z)$, which, from (3.11), can be written as

$$\gamma(x_B - \alpha). \tag{3.12}$$

If we postulate a linear external damage function, then $\gamma(Z) = g Z$, or $\gamma(x_B - \alpha) = g[x_B - \alpha]$.

3.5.2 Abatement costs

Reducing emissions from x_B to Z imposes an abatement cost $\xi(x_B, Z)$ on Blue, increasing in x_B and decreasing in Z. As special cases, the abatement cost may be an increasing function of the amount abated $\alpha = x_B - Z$, or a decreasing function of the emissions-to-consumption ratio Z/x_B. Here we adopt the abatement-cost function

$$\xi(x_B, Z) = 0.5q [x_B - Z]^2 = 0.5q\alpha^2, \tag{3.13}$$

where q is a positive parameter. The resource cost of producing good X is, as before, linear, with average and marginal cost equal to c.

The social surplus function now has as arguments, besides x_R, two of the three variables x_B, Z and α. It turns out that, given the abatement-cost function (3.13), it is convenient to use x_B and α. Accordingly, from (3.11), (3.12) and (3.13), we write the social surplus function as:

$$S(x_B, x_R, \alpha) := v_B(x_B) - cx_B - 0.5q\alpha^2 + v_R(x_R) - cx_R - \gamma(x_B - \alpha).$$

3.5.3 The surplus-maximizing solution

We write (x_B^*, x_R^*, α^*) for the surplus-maximizing solution. As before, the equation "$v_R'(x_R) = c$" yields x_R^*, equal to Red's consumption at the

---

[15] Besides the installation of emission filters, the costs of abatement may include the investment in newer technologies and the switch to cleaner techniques or sources of energy.

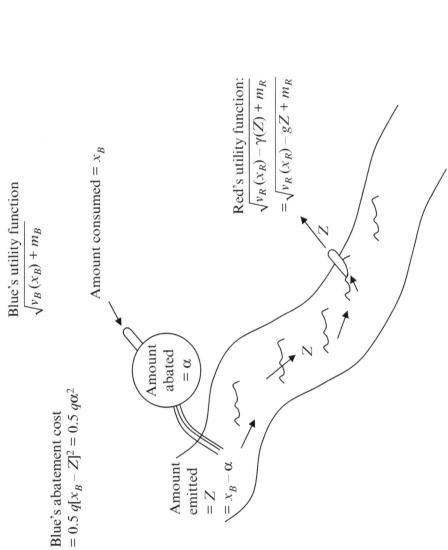

Figure 3.9 *Unidirectional negative externality with abatement*

free-market allocation, as it should be, because Red is still a passive recipient of the externality.

If abatement costs were very low, then surplus would be maximized at zero emissions. The analysis is simpler when this is not the case, i.e., when $x_B^* > \alpha^*$. Then x_B^* and α^* are found by setting to zero the derivatives (chain rule again) of surplus with respect to x_B and α, i.e., by solving,

$$v_B'(x_B) - c = \gamma'(x_B - \alpha), \tag{3.14}$$

and

$$q\alpha = \gamma'(x_B - \alpha). \tag{3.15}$$

The surplus-maximizing emission level is then defined as $Z^* = x_B^* - \alpha^*$.

If the external damage cost function is linear, namely, $\gamma(x_B - \alpha) = g[x_B - \alpha]$, then $\gamma'(x_B - \alpha) = g$, and (3.14)–(3.15) become

$$v_B'(x_B) - c = g, \tag{3.16}$$

$$q\alpha = g. \tag{3.17}$$

Equations (3.14) and (3.16) are interpreted as:

Marginal benefit from consumption − Marginal internal cost of consumption = Marginal external cost of consumption,

whereas (3.15) and (3.17) are interpreted as:

Marginal cost of abatement = Marginal benefit from abatement.

Note that the right-hand sides of (3.14) and (3.15) (or of (3.16) and (3.17)) are identical: in words, these equations imply that

*Marginal external damage by emissions =
Marginal benefit from emission abatement.*

Figure 3.10 illustrates the surplus-maximizing solution.

3.5.4   The free-market allocation and policy approaches

At the free-market allocation, Blue chooses x_B and α in order to maximize $v_B(x_B) - cx_B - 0.5q\alpha^2$. Blue inefficiently chooses $\tilde{\alpha} = 0$ (because

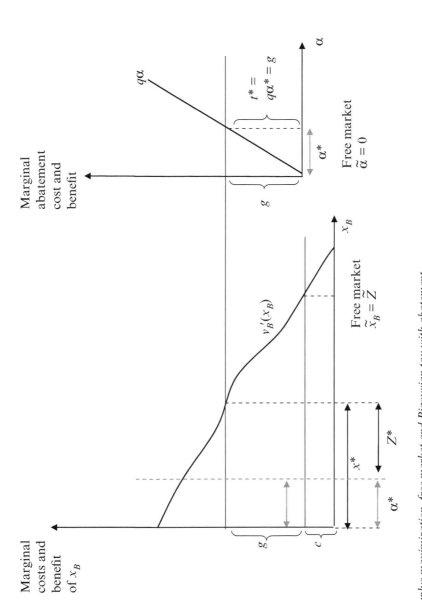

Figure 3.10 *Surplus maximization, free market and Pigouvian tax with abatement*

abatement is costly and returns no benefit to Blue) and consumption $\tilde{x}_B$ as the solution to

$$v_B'(x_B) = c. \tag{3.18}$$

see Figure 3.10. Clearly, $\tilde{x}_B > x_B^*$.

Interestingly, in order to induce efficiency, it is emissions Z, rather than consumption x_B or abatement α, that must be targeted by policy. Either quotas or Pigouvian taxes can be imposed on Z.

Efficient quota on emissions

Blue is prevented from emitting more than $Z^* = x_B^* - \alpha^*$ units. Then Blue chooses x_B and $Z \leq Z^*$ in order to maximize $v_B(x_B) - cx_B - 0.5q[x_B - Z]^2$. Because this expression is increasing in Z, Blue chooses $Z = Z^*$, hence emitting $Z^* = x_B^* - \alpha^*$ units. Her benefit is now

$$v_B(x_B) - cx_B - 0.5q[x_B - Z^*]^2,$$

maximized when x_B satisfies the first-order condition

$$v_B'(x_B) - c = q[x_B - Z^*],$$

an equation (with at most one solution) satisfied by the efficient consumption x_B^* because, from (3.16) and (3.17), we know that $v_B'(x_B^*) - c = q[x_B^* - Z^*]$. Thus, a quota on emissions at level Z^* induces surplus maximization.

Pigouvian tax on emissions

The marginal Pigouvian tax rate is, as usual, $t^* = g$, i.e., Blue pays the tax $t^* Z = t^*[x_B - \alpha]$. Then Blue chooses x_B and α in order to maximize $v_B(x_B) - cx_B - 0.5q\alpha^2 - t^*[x_B - \alpha]$. The first order conditions are

$$v_B'(x_B) - c = t^*,$$

$$q\alpha = t^*,$$

the same as (3.16) and (3.17). Hence, a Pigouvian tax rate on emissions with marginal rate $t^* = g$ induces surplus maximization, see Figure 3.10.

Inefficient policies

But targeting x_B or α does not yield the surplus-maximizing solution.

- *Setting a quota $\bar{x}_B$ on consumption x_B.* Blue then chooses $x_B \leq \bar{x}_B$ and α in order to maximize $v_B(x_B) - cx_B - 0.5q\alpha^2$. This expression decreases with α, and therefore Blue chooses $\tilde{\alpha} = 0 < \alpha^*$, no matter what $\bar{x}_B$ is. Hence, a quota on consumption cannot induce the social-surplus maximizing level of emissions or abatement.

- *Taxing consumption x_B at marginal rate $\bar{t}$.* Blue then chooses x_B and α in order to maximize $v_B(x_B) - cx_B - 0.5q\alpha^2 - \bar{t}x_B$. As just seen, this expression decreases with α, and therefore Blue chooses $\tilde{\alpha} = 0 < \alpha^*$, no matter what $\bar{t}$ is. Hence, a tax on consumption cannot lead to social surplus maximization either.

- *Setting minimum level, or floor, $\bar{\alpha}$ on abatement.* Again, Blue maximizes $v_B(x_B) - cx_B - 0.5q\alpha^2$, a function that is decreasing in α and hence she will choose $\alpha = \bar{\alpha}$. But if $\bar{\alpha}$ is set at α^*, then Blue will choose $\tilde{x}_B > x_B^* \geq \alpha^*$, which solves the first-order condition $v_B'(x_B) = c$. Hence, a floor on abatement cannot lead to social surplus maximization.

- *Subsidizing abatement at rate $\bar{s}$.* Now Blue chooses x_B and α in order to maximize $v_B(x_B) - cx_B - 0.5q\alpha^2 + \bar{s}\alpha$. Again, if the subsidy induces the abatement level α^*, then Blue will choose $\tilde{x}_B > x_B^* \geq \alpha^*$, inconsistent with social surplus maximization.

3.6 Bargaining

3.6.1 Disagreement points

We go back to Blue and Red of Section 3.2.1 above, with the following data.

Blue. Upstream, generator of the externality:
$$U_B(x_B, m_B) = \sqrt{v_B(x_B)} + m_B,$$

Red. Downstream, recipient of the externality:
$$U_R(x_R, Z, m_R) = \sqrt{v_R(x_R)} + m_R - \gamma(Z),$$

where $Z = x_B$.

Blue (resp. Red) is initially endowed with ω_B (resp. ω_R) units of numeraire.

For simplicity, let the resource cost of producing good X be zero, i.e., $c = 0$. As in 3.2.2 and 3.5.2 above, Red's free-market allocation coincides with its surplus-maximizing level x_R^*.

Perhaps Blue and Red may negotiate an efficient agreement. But if they do not agree, a point is reached that we call the *disagreement point*, determined by the legal system, by custom or by some not modeled characteristics of the participants (say, Red's ability to credibly threaten Blue). The disagreement point is typically inefficient.

We will consider alternative disagreement points corresponding to different legal rights or duties of the generator and the recipient of the externality, an approach pioneered by Coase. In other words, the inefficiency displayed by the disagreement point occurs within the limits of a given legal system.

3.6.2   The disagreement point when the recipient has no right to clean water

Assume that Red has no rights, and Blue can freely choose the level of x_B. (In the legal terminology of Wesley Hohfeld, Blue has the *liberty* of emitting.)[16] Unless there is an agreement, Blue chooses the quantity x_B that maximizes $v_B(x_B)$, namely the inefficient free-market amount $\tilde{x}_B$. (See Figure 3.2 above.) The resulting utilities are: $U_B = \sqrt{v_B(\tilde{x}_B)} + \omega_B$ and $U_R = \sqrt{v_R(x_R^*)} - \gamma(\tilde{x}_B) + \omega_R$, represented as point A in Figure 3.11.

3.6.3   The disagreement point when the recipient has the right to clean water

Assume now that Red has the right to clean water, and, thus, Blue has the duty not to emit. Red can exercise his rights and dictate the level of x_B. If he chooses x_B without agreement with Blue, he will impose the level of x_B that minimizes $\gamma(x_B)$, namely $x_B = 0$, an inefficient amount (see Figure 3.2). The resulting utilities will be: $U_B = \sqrt{\omega_B}$ and $U_R = \sqrt{v_R(x_R^*)} + \omega_R$, plotted as point B in Figure 3.11.

3.6.4   Complete bargaining

Suppose that Blue and Red fully cooperate and jointly agree on x_B, together with some transfers of money. The expressions "complete bargaining," "cooperation," or "absence of transaction costs" mean that the actors exhaust all possible gains from negotiation: they end up maximizing $v_B(x_B) - \gamma(x_B)$ and reaching a point on the utility possibility frontier, while agreeing on transfers that make nobody worse off than at the disagreement point. The final utility pair will depend on the

---

[16] I.e., Blue has no *duty* to refrain from or to limit the extent of externality-causing activity, and, hence, Blue has the *privilege* (or the *liberty*) to engage in the activities. The reference is Wesley N. Hohfeld (1919, 1978), *Fundamental Legal Conceptions as Applied to Judicial Reasoning*, edited by Walter W. Cook: Western, Connecticut: Greenwood Press. It should be noted that Hohfeld's terminology does not allow the use of the word "right" or "claim" here, because somebody's right must necessarily be accompanied by somebody else's duty.

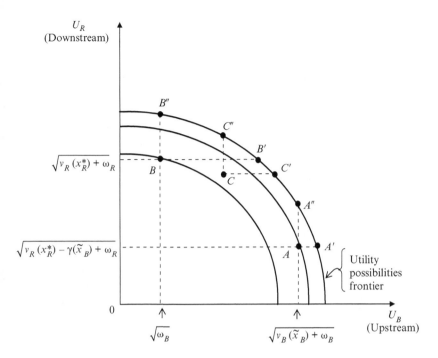

Figure 3.11   *Complete bargaining under alternative disagreement points*

bargaining process, but it must be between A' and A'' of Figure 3.11 if Red has no right to clean water, and between B' and B'' if he has the right.

Coase believed that complete bargaining is unlikely in practice: he thought that real-life "transaction costs" will often prevent the parties from reaching an efficient agreement. But he did discuss, as a reference point, the example of the cattle raiser and the farmer (corresponding to our Blue and Red) in the ideal situation of absence of transaction costs. Basically by definition, efficiency is reached in the absence of transaction costs. This statement is a version of the so-called Coase Theorem, see Appendix 3B below.

3.6.5 Pigouvian taxes plus complete bargaining

Suppose that Blue has no duty to keep the water clean, and that the policy maker imposes on Blue a tax at marginal rate $t^* = \gamma'(x^*)$. As seen in Section 3.2.5 above, if Blue makes her decision without agreement with Red (there are high "transaction costs"), then she chooses the efficient level x_B^*, because she maximizes:

$$v_B(x_B) - t^* x_B,$$

i.e., she solves the equation: $v_B'(x_B) = t^*$.

But suppose that the policy maker is mistaken in assuming that Blue and Red will not bargain, when in fact they do bargain completely. Then the outcome will be inefficient under the Pigouvian tax t^*, although it would still be efficient if the tax receipts are actually given (as a compensation) to Red.

The argument is simple. Consider complete bargaining, which means that the actors agree on maximizing the sum of the benefits accruing to them. If, as in Section 3.6.4 above, no taxes are imposed, then the bargainers maximize

$$v_B(x_B) - \gamma(x_B),$$

i.e., they choose the surplus-maximizing level x_B^*, solving the equation

$$v_B'(x_B) - \gamma'(x_B) = 0.$$

But if the tax is imposed on Blue and no compensation is paid to Red, then the complete bargainers maximize the sum of benefits accruing to them

$$v_B(x_B) - \gamma(x_B) - t^* x_B.$$

The chosen x_B is then too small, because it satisfies:

$$v_B'(x_B) = \gamma'(x_B) + t^*.$$

In a sense, the externality is doubly internalized through both complete bargaining and the Pigouvian tax.

Last, let the tax receipts $t^* x_B$ be actually transferred to Red. When the complete bargainers agree on maximizing the sum of the benefits accruing to them, they maximize

$$v_B(x_B) - \gamma(x_B) - t^* x_B + t^* x_B = v_B(x_B) - \gamma(x_B),$$

reaching efficiency.

Appendix 3A   Omnidirectional externalities in the continuum economy

3A.1   The model

Here we extend the continuum model of appendices 1A and 2A above to include omnidirectional externalities. Congestion and common-pool resources will be modeled by the *negative* externality, whereas the *positive* externality will be interpreted as a network.[17]

As in there, we have a continuum $(0, N_0]$ of *potential consumers of good X, users* or *participants in the externality-causing activity*, terms that we use interchangeably. In fact, the term "participant" is more suggestive than "consumer" in many of the applications: a person may decide to participate or not in a congestion-generating activity, or in the exploitation of a common pool resource, or in joining a network. As before, the set of active consumers or participants is an interval of the form $(0, N]$, the production cost of supplying good X to $(0, N]$, or of providing for a participation level N, is cN, and we order potential users by nondecreasing valuation of (one unit of) good X, or, in other words, by the value that they place on participating.

But now the valuation of good X by potential consumer n will depend on the *participation level N*. More specifically, we assume that user n's valuation of participating when the participation level is N is given by a function of the form $\bar{v}(n, N)$, increasing (resp. decreasing) in N when the externality is positive (resp. negative).

3A.2   Negative externality: congestion and the tragedy of the commons

Postulate the individual valuation function

$$\bar{v}(n, N) = [N_0 - N] [N_0 - \delta n], \tag{3A.1}$$

where the "diversity" parameter δ can be one or zero: given a participation level N, when $\delta = 1$, n's valuation is lower the higher her number n is, as in appendices 1A and 2A above; but when $\delta = 0$, all individuals have the same valuation.

At the participation level N, all persons with numbers n less than or equal to N participate, and their valuations can be aggregated as

---

[17] The continuum model is particularly adequate for omnidirectional externalities involving large numbers of generators, since the effect of the externality-causing activity by a generator on herself is then zero, rather than just negligible, as was the case in the North–South model of Section 3.3 above.

$$\int_0^N [N_0 - N][N_0 - \delta n] dn = [N_0 - N][N_0 \int_0^N dn - \delta \int_0^N n dn]$$

$$= [N_0 - N]\left[N_0 N - \frac{\delta}{2}N^2 \right].$$

Hence, the social surplus function is

$$S(N) = [N_0 - N]\left[N_0 N - \frac{\delta}{2}N^2 \right] - cN, \qquad (3A.2)$$

with marginal social surplus

$$S'(N) := -N_0 N + \frac{\delta}{2}N^2 + [N_0 - \delta N][N_0 - N] - c, \qquad (3A.3)$$

which must be zero at the surplus-maximizing N^* (as long as $N^* > 0$ and $N^* < N_0$).

In order to compute the free-market equilibrium, we first note that the equilibrium price of good X, or the price of participating, must equal c. A consumer participates if her valuation is not lower than the price. Hence the free-market participation level is defined by the equation

$$[N_0 - \delta N][N_0 - N] - c = 0. \qquad (3A.4)$$

The comparison of (3A.4) with (3A.3) shows that the marginal aggregate valuation $-N[N_0 - [\delta N/2]] + [N_0 - \delta N][N_0 - N]$, is lower than the valuation of the marginal consumer, $[N_0 - \delta N][N_0 - N]$.[18] Hence, if (3A.4) is satisfied at the free-market equilibrium, then (3A.3) is negative. It follows that the market equilibrium participation level is inefficiently high, as we should expect in the presence of a negative externality.

Let us simplify the analysis to the case of $c = 0$ (zero costs) and identical consumers ($\delta = 0$). From (3A.1), the individual valuation is

$$\bar{v}(n, N) = [N_0 - N]N_0, \qquad (3A.5)$$

and from (3A.2), social surplus is now

$$S(N) = [N_0 - N]N_0 N, \qquad (3A.6)$$

see Figure 3A.1(a). Social surplus is maximized when the marginal surplus

$$S'(N) = -N_0 N + N_0[N_0 - N] = [N_0]^2 - 2N_0 N \qquad (3A.7)$$

is zero, i.e., $N^* = N_0/2$. But aggregate indirect demand is instead given by

[18] Note that, because $\delta \leq 1$ and $N \leq N_0$, the term $[N_0 - [\delta N/2]]$ is positive.

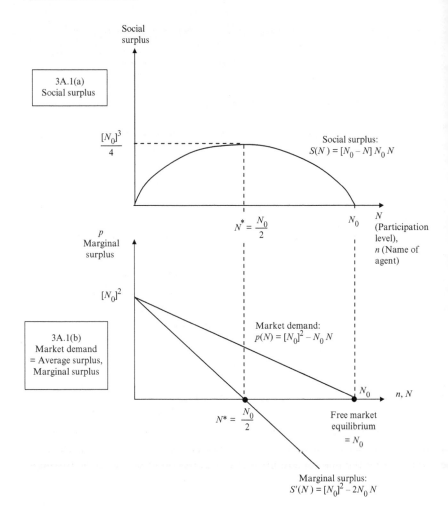

Figure 3A.1   *The tragedy of the commons in the continuum economy*

$p(N) = N_0[N_0 - N] = [N_0]^2 - N_0N$. Market equilibrium occurs when $p(N) = 0$, i.e., when $N = N_0$, with

$$v(n, N_0) = 0, \qquad (3A.8)$$

for all n! This is a striking illustration of the inefficiency of the free-market equilibrium in the presence of externalities.

One interpretation of the model is congestion: by entering a busy freeway you slow down all traffic. The extreme case of (3A.8) corresponds to all traffic stopped.

The model can also be interpreted as that of a production omnidirectional externality, such as a common pool resource, exploited by a large number of independent agents or firms. As discussed in Section 3.1 above, the resource may be a fishery, oilfield or an aquifer. Hardin (1968) used the example of the common grazing range to emphasize the case where, in the absence of policy intervention or collective action, the access to the resource is open, resulting in an inefficient outcome, which he called the "tragedy of the commons."[19]

Common-pool resources may be modeled in various ways: Appendix 1B above presented a game with two persons, each having two strategies available to her (six cows vs. eight cows). Alternatively, we could consider a finite number of participants each of whom can choose any nonnegative number (interpreted as, say, effort) as a strategy. This section interprets the model of (3A.5), with $c = 0$, as that of a fishery. There is a continuum, $(0, N_0]$, of potential, identically productive fishers.[20] A fisher has two possible strategies: Active and Inactive. The catch of an active fisher depends on the participation level N and is given by (3A.5): this is also the *average* catch per active fisher. The total catch is given by (3A.6), with *marginal* catch given by (3A.7), lower than the average catch: see Figure 3A.1(b).

Total catch would be maximized if the marginal catch were zero, implying that half of the fishers are inactive. But as long as the average catch is positive, additional fishers have the incentive to become active, and the free-market equilibrium occurs when all potential fishers are active, i.e., $N = N_0$. This results in a nil catch, evoking Hardin's (1968, p. 1244) words,

> Ruin is the destination towards which all men rush, each pursuing his own best interest in a society that believes in the freedom of the commons.

The commons externality is of the production–production type. Besides the policies of taxes and permits studied in the main text for

---

[19] G. Hardin (1968), "The tragedy of the commons," *Science*, 162, 1243–1248.
[20] By letting $\delta = 1$ in (3A.1) we would capture the more complex case where some fishers are more productive than others.

consumption externalities, we now have an alternative policy, that we call *merger* or *privatization*: a single firm is given exclusive ownership of the resource, here the fishery, and controls all the productive activities that use the fishery. Note that this approach cannot be applied to consumption externalities: one can merge many firms into one, but one cannot "merge" many people into a single person.

Because ownership may become concentrated under privatization, it may be objectionable from the distributional viewpoint: it all depends on how profits are distributed. Moreover, if the privatized firm enjoyed any monopoly power, then the outcome would not be efficient.[21] Otherwise, if the privatized firm is a perfect competitor in the fish market, then it takes the market price p_F of fish as given, and chooses N as to maximize total profits, i.e., total revenue, given that costs are zero.[22] Thus, it chooses N as to maximize total catch (multiplied by the price of fish), i.e., (from (3A.6)), it maximizes $p_F [N_0 - N]N_0 N$, and hence it chooses the efficient level $N^* = N_0/2$, with total catch $[N_0]^3/4$ and profits:

$$\text{Profits of the privatized firm} = p_F \frac{[N_0]^3}{4}. \qquad (3A.9)$$

Note that (3A.9) can be interpreted as the (market) value of the fishery. We now show that the same value appears under the alternative interpretations based on the policy approaches discussed in the main text. Let us return to the independent fishers.

The inefficiency of the free-market, or free-access, equilibrium is due to the fact that, as long as the average catch is positive, there is entry in the fishery. But assume that the public authority imposes a Pigouvian fishing fee or tax t^*: each potential fisher is free to engage in fishing as long as she pays t^*. For efficiency, the tax should be low enough so that, when the participation level is N^*, no active fisher finds it profitable to quit fishing and save the tax amount t^*, i.e., $p_F N_0 [N_0 - N^*] \geq t^*$; on the other hand, it should be high enough not to encourage inactive fishers to become active, i.e., $p_F N_0 [N_0 - N^*] \leq t^*$. Summarizing, the Pigouvian tax rate is $t^* = p_F N_0 [N_0 - N^*]$ which, by the definition of N^*, can be written $t^* = p_F N_0 [N_0 - N_0/2]$, i.e.,

$$t^* = p_F \frac{[N_0]^2}{2}. \qquad (3A.10)$$

---

[21] With monopoly power, the firm would no longer face a constant fish price, but a downward sloping demand curve. Thus, in accordance with standard monopoly theory, it would choose a catch lower than the competitive firm, i.e., lower than the maximal, efficient catch.

[22] Of course, under competitive conditions, p_F is the marginal social valuation of fish.

At this rate, the participation level is exactly $N^* = N_0/2$, generating the aggregate tax receipts:

$$\text{Pigouvian tax receipts} = p_F \frac{[N_0]^3}{4},$$

the same as (3A.9), i.e., *the Pigouvian tax receipts equal the profits of the (competitive) firm in the merge policy.*

Section 3.2.5 above interprets the Pigouvian tax rate as the marginal external damage. A similar interpretation is valid here. From (3A.5), the rate of change of individual profit as the participation level increases is $d(p_F[N_0 - N]N_0)/dN = -p_F N_0$. At the efficient participation level, all fishers in the interval $(0, N^*] = (0, N_0/2]$ are affected. Multiplying the individual marginal external damage by the participation level N^* yields $p_F[N_0]^2/2$, which is precisely the Pigouvian tax rate given by (3A.10). Hence the Pigouvian tax rate reflects the *incremental aggregate damage that the marginal fisher imposes on all other fishers.*

The Pigouvian tax rate can also be interpreted here as the difference, evaluated at efficient participation level, between average revenue (average catch multiplied by the price of fish), which is $p_F[N_0 - N^*]N_0 = p_F[N_0]^2/2$, and marginal revenue (marginal catch multiplied by the price of fish), which is zero: this corresponds to the vertical distance between the two curves of Figure 3A.1(b) at $N^* = N_0/2$, multiplied by p_F. Hence the Pigouvian tax rate fills the gap between the *marginal social benefit and the benefit of the marginal fisher*, here equal to the *average profit.*

Consider now a cap-and-trade system. The supply of permits is fixed at the activity level N^*. What will be the equilibrium price, denoted r^*, of a permit? Suppose that you do not have a permit. If you buy one, you will go fishing and catch $[N_0 - N^*]N_0 = [N_0]^2/2$ fish that you will sell for $p_F[N_0]^2/2$. If the price r of a permit were less than $p_F[N_0]^2/2$, then everybody without a permit would like to buy one, and, thus, the demand for permits would exceed supply. Thus, the equilibrium price r^* of a permit must satisfy $r^* \geq p_F[N_0]^2/2$. Now suppose that you do have a permit. If you sell it, you would obtain r units of numeraire, while if you keep and use it you obtain $p_F[N_0]^2/2$. If $r > p_F[N_0]^2/2$, then everybody with a permit would like to sell it. This would not be an equilibrium either. Thus $r^* \leq p_F[N_0]^2/2$. Putting these two inequalities together we obtain as the market-equilibrium price of a permit $r^* = p_F[N_0]^2/2$, the same as the Pigouvian tax rate. The total market value of the permits issued is then $[N_0/2]p_F[N_0]^2/2 = p_F[N_0]^3/4$, as in (3A.9), which again can be interpreted as the value of the fishery.

3A.3   Positive externality: the network

Consider a network such as a communications system (telephone, e-mail, language) or a standard to be adopted. The basic idea of the network externality is that the usefulness of joining the network or adopting the standard depends on how many people do the same. Hence, anyone's decision to participate creates a positive, omnidirectional externality on all other users.

We now consider the individual valuation function

$$\bar{v}(n, N) = N[N_0 - n].$$

Social surplus is computed as in (3A.2) above as

$$S(N) := \int_0^N N[N_0 - n]dn - cN = N\left[N_0N - \frac{1}{2}N^2\right] - cN, \quad (3A.11)$$

with marginal surplus

$$S'(N) = N_0N - \frac{1}{2}N^2 + [N_0 - N]N - c = N_0N - \frac{1}{2}N^2 + N_0N - N^2 - c$$

$$= 2N_0N - \frac{3}{2}N^2 - c,$$

which for reasonable values of c (see discussion below) is positive at $N = N_0$, in which case efficiency requires everybody to participate in the network: this can be accomplished with a subsidy equal to the marginal cost c, making the participation in the network free. (The marginal participant is then N_0, who is then indifferent between participating and not participating, because $[N_0 - N_0]N - c + c = 0$.) See Figure 3A.2, where the marginal surplus equals the (graphed) marginal social valuation minus the marginal social cost c.

We now turn to the free market. Let a price p be charged for participating in the network. The valuation of the network by potential user n, namely $N[N_0 - n]$, is then her *reservation price*: when the participation level is N, potential user n wishes to participate if the market price p is less than $N[N_0 - n]$ and does not wish to participate if $p > N[N_0 - n]$. Note that if $N = 0$, then $[N_0 - n]N = 0$, i.e., nobody has any use for a network without participants, and nobody wishes to pay a positive price for participating. Thus, $N = 0$ is a possible participation level demanded at any price.

We have two other possible levels of participation demanded if the price p is not too high. Note that $N > 0$ is a participation level demanded at price p if, given N:

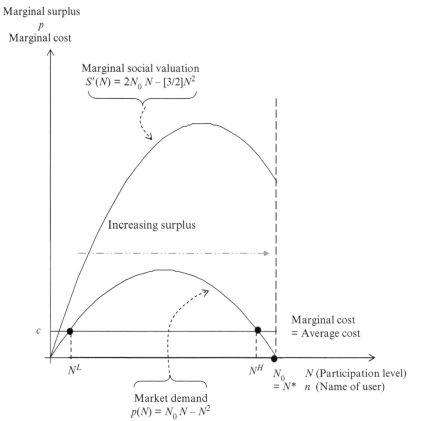

Figure 3A.2   *Network externality in the continuum economy*

- Everybody in the interval $(0, N)$ wishes to participate, i.e., $p < N[N_0 - n]$, for $n < N$;
- Nobody in the interval $(N, N_0]$ wishes to participate, i.e., $p > N[N_0 - n]$, for $n > N$;
- Hence, $p = N[N_0 - n]$, for $n = N$: in other words, the potential user with name or number N is just indifferent between participating or not: we call her the *marginal user*.

Thus, the market demand curve is given by

- either $N = 0$,
- or $N > 0$ and $p = N_0 N - N^2$,

see Figure 3A.2.

Summarizing, $N > 0$ is a participation level consistent with market demand at price p if and only if N solves the equation

$$N^2 - N_0 N + p = 0, \tag{3A.12}$$

which has the two solutions

$$N = \frac{N_0 \pm \sqrt{[N_0]^2 - 4p}}{2}.$$

Of course, if $p = 0$, then the two solutions to (3A.12) are zero and N_0.

The market supply curve is horizontal at level c. If c is not too high, the marginal cost curve intersects the demand curve at three points, which we call the *zero equilibrium* ($N = 0$), the *low-level equilibrium* (N^L) and the *high-level equilibrium* (N^H): see Figure 3A.2.

The low-level equilibrium is unstable in the following sense. Starting from it, suppose that the price stays at c but there is a random deviation in the degree of participation, so that the interval of participants becomes $(0, N^L + \varepsilon]$, where e is a small positive number, instead of the original $(0, N^L]$. The valuation (or reservation price) of the marginal user, indicated by the ordinate of the demand curve, is then higher than the market price: thus, more potential users participate. Eventually, a random deviation to the right of N^L leads to point N^H. By the same argument, a left deviation from N^L would lead to zero, whereas any small deviation from N^H would lead back to N^H.

We conclude that there are two stable equilibria, zero and the high-level equilibrium, and an unstable one, namely the low-level equilibrium. The magnitude N^L can be interpreted as a critical mass. If the network fails to attract at least an interval of length N^L, then it falls into the "zero trap" and fails to survive.

It can be seen in Figure 3A.2 that, for N large enough, the marginal social valuation is above the marginal cost curve, so that surplus increases with the participation level.[23] As anticipated above, maximal surplus is achieved at the boundary where $N = N_0$, when everybody participates in the network, and all three free market equilibria entail an inefficiently low participation level. The second-best problem of maximizing surplus without subsidization is equivalent to the choice of the best market equilibrium among the three, which corresponds to the participation level N^H. This may require some once-and-for-all policy intervention to launch the network and push it past the critical mass N^L, thus avoiding the zero-equilibrium trap.

---

[23] The maximum value of the branch of the demand curve $p = N_0 N - N^2$, achieved at $N = N_0/2$, is $[N_0]^2/4$. Thus, if there is a market equilibrium with positive N, one must have $c \leq [N_0]^2/4$ (otherwise the horizontal line at level c would not intersect the curve $p = N_0 N - N^2$, and zero would be the only market equilibrium). But the marginal aggregate valuation at N_0 is $2[N_0]^2 - [3/2][N_0]^2 = [N_0]^2/2 > [N_0]^2/4$. Thus, the marginal aggregate valuation at N_0 is higher than the marginal cost c whenever a market equilibrium with positive N exists.

Appendix 3B   The so-called Coase theorem

3B.1   Statements

I say "so-called Coase Theorem" because this is precisely Coase's own phrase.[24] He never stated the "theorem," but textbooks offer some statements. Jonathan Gruber (*Public Finance and Public Policy*, 2nd Edition, New York: Worth, 2007, p. 130) writes:

> Part I of the Coase Theorem: when there are well-defined property rights and costless bargaining, then negotiations between the party creating the externality and the party affected by the externality can bring about the socially optimal market quantity.

As another instance, Joseph Stiglitz (*Economics of the Public Sector*, 3rd Edition, New York: Norton, 2000, p. 219), writes

> The assertion that whenever there are externalities, the parties involved can get together and make some set of arrangements by which the externality is internalized and efficiency is ensured, is referred to as the Coase Theorem.

Harvey Rosen (*Public Finance*, Homewood, IL: Irwin, 1992, p.105) writes:

> The conclusion is that the efficient solution will be achieved *independently* of who is assigned the property rights as long as *someone* is assigned these rights. This result, known as the Coase Theorem, implies that, once property rights are established, no government intervention is needed to deal with externalities.

The "Coase Theorem" suggests noninterventionist policies: the parties will meet and implement by themselves an efficient solution, so that no government policy is required. Coase himself was skeptical of this line of argument, because he did not believe in the practical relevance of the "absence of transaction costs" assumption. His own arguments for nonintervention display a second-best character.

It should be noted that, if bargaining is truly costless, then complete bargainers should be able to reach an efficient allocation whether property rights are assigned or not. Whether the disagreement point is determined by law, as are points A and B in Figure 3.11, or by personal characteristics, as say point C, in the absence of "transaction costs" all potential

---

[24] See R.H. Coase (1988), *The Firm, the Market and the Law*, Chicago: University of Chicago Press, p. 13. He also wrote: "This is the infamous Coase theorem, named and formulated by George Stigler, although it is based on work of mine" (p. 716 in "The institutional structure of production," *American Economic Review*, 82(4), 1992, 713–719).

gains from negotiation should be exhausted, and a point on the utility possibilities frontier reached (say, between C' and C'' if the disagreement point is C).

3B.2   The second best when bargaining is impossible

Suppose that, unfortunately, bargaining is costly and Blue and Red cannot be expected to overcome the inefficiency of the disagreement point (in Coase's expression, there are large "transaction costs"). Suppose also that the policy maker is incapable of finding and implementing a policy of quotas, permits or taxes, and that it can only decide, by specifying rights and duties, the disagreement point. Then second-best surplus maximization requires Red to have the right to clean water if and only if $v_B(\tilde{x}_B) < \gamma(\tilde{x}_B)$. Of course, the inequality can in principle go either way: in Figure 3.11, for instance, the utility mini-frontier through point B lies below that of point A, which corresponds to the case where $v_B(\tilde{x}_B) > \gamma(\tilde{x}_B)$ and, accordingly, second-best surplus maximization requires Red not to have the right to clean water.

3B.3   Liability for damages

The disagreement point may take the following intermediate form: Blue can choose the level of emissions without Red's acquiescence, but Blue must compensate Red for any emission-caused losses, no more, no less. This is quite different from a Pigouvian tax scheme, where the government collects the tax and distributes the receipts in a lumpsum manner. But, depending on the particulars of the problem, it may (or may not) have the same effect.

The crucial consideration is whether the surplus-maximizing solution requires the recipient to mitigate the externality. Let Red have access to a mitigation technology, say, drilling a well rather than drink the polluted river water. If Red should drill the well at the surplus-maximizing solution, then Blue's liability for damages removes Red's incentives for drilling the well, and inefficiency occurs. (Note that the Pigouvian tax would be zero if surplus maximization entailed no abatement by Blue.) If, on the contrary, the surplus-maximizing solution requires Red not to drill the well, then the compensation by Blue does not alter Red's behavior, and Blue's liability has the same effect as the Pigouvian tax.

4 Public goods

● ●

4.1 Concepts

4.1.1 Nonrivalness

A good or service is *public* if its availability to one consumer does not preclude its availability to others, i.e., the good is *nonrival in consumption*.[1] In its pure form, nonrivalness in consumption means that the amount available to a person does not decrease when an extra person uses the good. More generally, if little extra cost is required to make the good available to an additional person, then consumption is to some extent nonrival.

Examples of highly nonrival goods
    National defense;
    Software;
    Radio signals;
    Global positioning system (GPS);
    TV broadcasts;
    Lighthouses;
    Weather forecasts;
    Information in general;
    Uncrowded facilities and natural environments.
Examples of goods with some degree of nonrivalness (congestion)[2]
    Crowded facilities and environments;
    Libraries;
    Fire protection;
    Police protection;
    Court system;
    Telephone networks;
    The internet;
    Wilderness areas.
Rival goods: All *private goods*: apples, gasoline, . . ., for which a person's consumption depletes the amount that can be made available to others.
    Note that some public goods (such as TV broadcasts) are provided by

---

[1] We use the term "a public good" for a particular good or service, not to be confused with the expressions "the public good" or "the common good," sometimes used to denote what here may be called "social welfare."

[2] Congestion is a form of negative externality: see Chapter 3.

the private sector, whereas some private goods are provided by the public sector (such as electricity in some areas).

4.1.2 Excludability

There is a second characteristic that may or may not be displayed by a public good, namely the *excludability* or *possibility of exclusion*. A public good is *excludable* if the provider can prevent particular persons from accessing it. As in the concept of nonrivalness, excludability is in practice a matter of degree: excluding some potential users may be feasible, but costly. In other instances, exclusion may be physically possible, but morally unacceptable.

Some public goods, such as national defense or clean air, are not excludable. Exclusion is possible for some public goods: a public park may be fenced in, the fire department may not answer calls from nonsubscribers and TV may be supplied by cable. If exclusion is possible, then different amounts of the public good may be made available to different people, i.e., $x_i \leq x$, with possibly $x_i < x$, for some Person i, where x denotes the amount produced and x_i the amount made available to Person i. For instance, a cable TV company may produce x programs, but make only $x_i < x$ of them available to basic subscribers.

If exclusion is feasible, then users may be charged *user fees*: The public good can then be supplied and financed through a market mechanism. The supplier can then be a government agency, a public firm, a private nonprofit firm, or even a profit-maximizing firm.[3]

4.1.3 Free disposal

A different property is that of *free disposal*, defined as the *ability of a person to access the public good in an amount lower than the amount made available to her*. For instance, the fact that she can access 24 hours of TV programming a day does not mean that she must spend all her life in front of the tube.

Under free disposal, a person may decide to access an amount $\tilde{x}_i$ of the public good *lower* than the amount x_i or capacity made available to her, i.e., it may be that $\tilde{x}_i < x_i$. An example of a public good for which there is no free disposal is national defense: you cannot reduce the protection offered by the US Navy, and your "use" of the US Navy equals the total amount available.

So far we have been considering public *goods*, i.e., goods or services

---

[3] Although there may be room for only a few firms, in which case perfect competition will not obtain, and regulation may be desirable.

that are desirable for everybody, or at least for a majority of people. (You may consider a freeway a "bad" if runs close to your bedroom window.) One could extend the concept to cover public "bads," such as salt in irrigation water, polluted air, traffic noise: these are the result of negative externalities, see Chapter 3. But we may note that the disposal of public bads is costly: every person is forced to "consume" the amount of the public bad that she faces, unless she engages in costly mitigation or abatement activities.

Conversely, no good can be "bad" under free disposal: at worst it is "neutral," because the consumer can choose to access it partially, or not at all. For an illustration, suppose that a person's utility function is

$$\tilde{U}_i(\tilde{x}_i, m_i) = \sqrt{8\tilde{x}_i - 0.5[\tilde{x}_i]^2 + m_i},$$

where $\tilde{x}_i$ is the number of hours per day that she spends in front of the TV, and m_i is her consumption of numeraire. In other words, $\tilde{v}_i(\tilde{x}_i) = 8\tilde{x}_i - 0.5[\tilde{x}_i]^2$ is her valuation function with the *actual number of viewing hours* as argument. We note that the marginal valuation of $\tilde{x}_i$ is $\tilde{v}_i'(\tilde{x}_i) = 8 - \tilde{x}_i$, negative for $\tilde{x}_i > 8$, for which quantities watching TV is, at the margin, a bad.

But under free disposal she will restrict her viewing to eight hours a day, even when more than eight hours are made available to her. Thus, if we use as argument in her utility function the *capacity* x_i of hours made available to her (instead of the number $\tilde{x}_i$ of hours *actually accessed*), then her utility function becomes

$$U_i(x_i, m_i) = \begin{cases} \sqrt{8x_i - 0.5[x_i]^2 + m_i}, & \text{if } x_i \le 8, \\ \sqrt{32 + m_i}, & \text{if } x_i > 8, \end{cases}$$

with (total) valuation function

$$v_i(x_i) = \begin{cases} 8x_i - 0.5[x_i]^2, & \text{if } x_i \le 8, \\ 32, & \text{if } x_i > 8, \end{cases}$$

and marginal valuation function

$$v_i'(x_i) = \begin{cases} 8 - x_i, & \text{if } x_i < 8, \\ 0, & \text{if } x_i > 8. \end{cases} \tag{4.1}$$

In other words, the marginal valuation functions, with the capacity available to the person as argument, are necessarily nonnegative under free disposal: marginal valuation of capacity is zero if the consumer prefers not to fully utilize it.

4.1.4 Summary

We may in principle distinguish among three magnitudes

x, the amount of the public good *produced* (*provided* or *supplied*),
x_i, the amount of the public good (or capacity) *available to Person i*,
$\tilde{x}_i$, the amount of the public good *accessed by Person i*.

It is always true that $\tilde{x}_i \leq x_i \leq x$.

If the good is *nonexcludable*, then we must have $\tilde{x}_i \leq x_i = x$, but, if the good is *excludable*, then we may have $\tilde{x}_i \leq x_i < x$. If there is *no free disposal*, then we must have $\tilde{x}_i = x_i \leq x$, but, if there is *free disposal*, then we may have $\tilde{x}_i < x_i \leq x$.

Examples

Nonexcludable, no free disposal: national defense.
Nonexcludable, free disposal: lighthouses, many forms of information.
Excludable, free disposal: cable TV.

It is hard to find examples of an *excludable* public good for which there is no *free disposal*.

In what follows, we will not write the actual amount accessed $\tilde{x}_i$ in the utility or valuation functions. If there is no free disposal, then $\tilde{x}_i = x_i$ anyway, and if there is free disposal, then we appeal to the discussion in Section 4.1.3 above. Accordingly, we shall typically write the public-good argument in *i*'s utility function as x, or possibly as x_i if the public good is excludable.

4.2   The efficient provision of public goods

4.2.1   Feasible states and efficiency

Under complete nonrivalness, even it exclusion is feasible, it would be inefficient to exclude some people who value the public good, or to restrict the access to it by individuals who have positive marginal valuations. Thus, the analysis of efficiency does not lose any generality if we assume that the same amount x is made available to all individuals, even when the public good is excludable, because then there is in all likelihood free disposal.

We follow the modeling of the public-good economy presented in Chapter 1. There are two goods, namely the public good and the numeraire, and I people. Person *i*'s utility function is written $U_i(x, m_i)$, where $x \geq 0$ is the amount of the public good provided and m_i is the amount of the numeraire good that Person i ends up with. The technology is described by a cost function $C(x)$ (i.e., $C(x)$ is the amount of numeraire required to produce x units of the public good), and the amount of the numeraire initially available is denoted ω. A *state of the economy* (or allocation) is a list of $I + 1$ numbers $(x, m_1, \ldots, m_I)$. A state is feasible if $C(x) + m_1 + \ldots, + m_I \leq \omega$, and a state satisfies *production efficiency* if $C(x) + m_1 + \ldots, + m_I = \omega$. But a new condition, called the Samuelson condition, will replace marginal efficiency conditions of the private good case.[4]

4.2.2   Efficiency condition for a Yes–No public good

To motivate the new condition, consider a Yes–No, or dichotomous, public good, say a bridge of a given design, and let society be comprised of two people: Blue and Red. Society has to decide whether to build it ($x = 1$) or not to build ($x = 0$). Let $\overline{C}$ denote the cost of building it (with the cost of not building equal to zero), and denote by $\overline{v}_B$ and $\overline{v}_R$, respectively, Blue's and Red's valuation of the bridge. (The valuations of "no bridge" are zero.) We argue that if, $\overline{v}_B + \overline{v}_R > \overline{C}$, then efficiency implies building the bridge. Indeed, suppose that $\overline{v}_B + \overline{v}_R > \overline{C}$, yet the bridge is not built. We can then find "taxes" A_B and A_R for Blue and Red, respectively, such that: $A_B < \overline{v}_B, A_R < \overline{v}_R$, and $A_B + A_R = \overline{C}$, i.e., it would be feasible to build the bridge and allocate its costs in such a way that both persons gain. Thus, not building the bridge is inefficient.[5] Similarly, if $\overline{v}_B + \overline{v}_R < \overline{C}$, then efficiency requires not to build the bridge.

The generalization to many people is straightforward. Let there be I persons, numbered 1 to I, and let $\overline{v}_i$ be i's valuation of the indivisible public good. Then:

Efficiency requires that the bridge be built if $\sum_{i=1}^{I} \overline{v}_i > \overline{C}$, *and*

Efficiency requires that the bridge not be built if $\sum_{i=1}^{I} \overline{v}_i < \overline{C}$.   (4.2)

---

[4] Named after Paul A. Samuelson (1915–2009), see his articles in the *Review of Economics and Statistics*, "The pure theory of public expenditure" (vol. 36, 1954, pp. 387–389) and "Diagrammatic exposition of a pure theory of public expenditure" (vol. 37, 1955, pp. 350–356). Samuelson was awarded the Nobel Prize in Economic Sciences in 1970.

[5] Strictly speaking, the argument requires that at the initial state both individuals be allocated a large enough amount of the numeraire good, so that they do not end up with a negative amount of numeraire, but we disregard this qualification, as we did in footnote 18 of Chapter 1 above.

4.2.3 Differentiability and the Samuelson condition

The logic of the previous argument can be extended to the case where the amount x of the public good is a continuous variable, and the utility functions are differentiable, yielding the equality, know as the *Samuelson condition*,

$$\sum_{i=1}^{I} |MRS_i(x, m_i)| = C'(x), \tag{4.3}$$

where the *marginal rate of substitution*, $MRS_i(x, m_i)$ is the slope of i's indifference curve at the point (x, m_i), i.e., with x on the horizontal axis.[6] Next, we explore the Samuelson condition for quasilinear preferences.

4.2.4 Quasilinear preferences and surplus maximization

As we did in previous chapters, we assume that Person i's utility function is $U_i(x, m_i) = \sqrt{v_i(x)} + m_i$, where $v_i(x)$ as Person i's *valuation of* (or i's *willingness to pay for*, or i's *benefit from*) x *units of the public good*. If we restrict the discussion to two people, Ms. Blue and Mr. Red, then, as we saw in Chapter 1, an allocation or state of the economy consists of three numbers, x, m_B and m_R, and economic efficiency requires production efficiency together with the maximization of social surplus.

Recall that *Social surplus* := *Sum of valuations – Cost,* which here becomes

$$S(x) := v_B(x) + v_R(x) - C(x).$$

Thus, *at an efficient allocation* (x^*, m_B, m_R), *the amount of public good* x^* *must maximize* $S(x)$. The principle of surplus maximization applies whether the public good is divisible or indivisible. In fact, conditions (4.2) are equivalent to the maximization of surplus for a Yes–No public good,

---

[6] Using partial derivatives,

$$MRS_i(x, m_i) = -\frac{\dfrac{\partial U_i(x, m_i)}{\partial x}}{\dfrac{\partial U_i(x, m_i)}{\partial m_i}},$$

and the Samuelson condition reads

$$\sum_{i=1}^{I} \frac{\dfrac{\partial U_i(x, m_i)}{\partial x}}{\dfrac{\partial U_i(x, m_i)}{\partial m_i}} = C'(x).$$

because then the surplus of not supplying the bridge is zero, while that of supplying it is $\Sigma_{i=1}^{I} \bar{v}_i - \overline{C}$.

On the other hand, let the public good be a continuous variable, and let all functions be differentiable. Suppose that x^* maximizes social surplus. Then (if $x^* > 0$) the derivative of S must be zero at x^*. For two quasilinear people, this condition implies

$$v_B'(x^*) + v_R'(x^*) = C'(x^*). \tag{4.4}$$

In words, the marginal cost of providing the public good must equal the sum of the "marginal valuations" or "marginal benefits." The Samuelson Condition (4.3) now takes the form (4.4).

We can argue (4.4) as we did (4.2). Suppose that one of our friends, a contrarian, does not believe that the Samuelson condition must hold at an efficient allocation. In fact, he claims to have found an efficient allocation where $v_B'(x) + v_R'(x) > C'(x)$, for instance, $v_B'(x) = 3$, $v_R'(x) = 6$ and $C'(x) = 7$. We can persuade him as follows. Starting at the allocation that he "found," let us produce one extra (small) unit of the public good. The additional amount of numeraire required is about seven units: perhaps we can take two units of numeraire from Blue's pocket, and five more units from Red's pocket. How does this impact the welfare of the two individuals?

Blue gets to enjoy an extra unit of the public good, which she values at 3, and has two units of numeraire, which she values at 2, withdrawn from her pocket. Thus, she prefers the new allocation to the previous one.

Red gets to enjoy an extra unit of the public good, which he values at 6, and has five units of numeraire, which he values at 5, withdrawn from his pocket. Thus, he prefers the new allocation to the previous one. In summary, this is a win–win change, and, therefore, the allocation proposed by our friend is not efficient. We can tell him: sorry, but you probably got confused.

The argument can be expressed in graphical terms as follows. Figure 4.1(a) plots Blue's marginal valuation of the public good. It is drawn as a straight line, corresponding to a quadratic valuation function $v_B(x)$ that has a maximum at the level x_B^0 of the public good. We postulate that for $x > x_B^0$, Blue's marginal valuation is zero, i.e., if $x > x_B^0$ units of the public good are made available to Blue, then she accesses only x_B^0 of them: the remaining units, $x - x_B^0$, neither benefit nor hurt Blue: this is the free disposal assumption, and her utility, valuation and marginal valuation functions are of the type leading to (4.1).

Formally, Figure 4.1(a) corresponds to a valuation function that is flat to the right of x_B^0, i.e.,

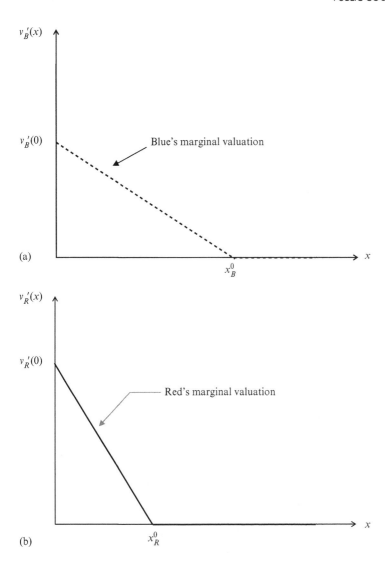

Figure 4.1   *Marginal valuations of a public good by two consumers (with free disposal)*

$$v_B(x) = \begin{cases} a_B x - \dfrac{b_B}{2} x^2 & \text{if } x \leq \dfrac{a_B}{b_B} := x_B^0, \\[2ex] \dfrac{1}{2} \dfrac{[a_B]^2}{b_B} & \text{otherwise,} \end{cases}$$

with marginal valuation function

$$v_B'(x) = \begin{cases} a_B - b_B x & \text{if } x < \dfrac{a_B}{b_B} := x_B^0, \\[1ex] 0 & \text{if } x > x_B^0 \end{cases}$$

as in (4.1) above.

Similarly, we draw in Figure 4.1(b) Red's marginal valuation. The Samuelson condition requires that, at the quantity x^* consistent with efficiency:

$$v_B'(x^*) + v_R'(x^*) = C'(x^*),$$

see Figure 4.2. The left term is the vertical sum of the two curves in Figure 4.1. The intersection of this vertical sum with the marginal cost curve determines x^*.

In Figure 4.2, the marginal cost is relatively high, and at x^* both marginal valuations are positive. But if the marginal cost were lower, then Red's marginal valuation could be zero at x^*. This situation is illustrated in Figure 4.3. Under free disposal, it does not matter which is the amount of the public good made available to Red, as long as it is not lower than x_R^0.

The analysis can be easily extended to any number of quasilinear people. Let $v_i(x)$ be i's valuation function, for $i = 1,. . ., I$. Then social surplus is $\Sigma_{i=1}^{I} v_i(x) - C(x)$. Setting its derivative equal to zero yields the Samuelson condition

$$\sum_{i=1}^{I} v_i'(x) = C'(x).$$

The utility possibilities frontier for the two-people case is similar to the one in Section 2.2 above: an arc of the circle centered at zero with radius $\sqrt{S^* + \omega}$, where S^* is the maximal surplus.

4.2.5 Comparison of the marginal conditions for efficiency in public and private goods

Feasible allocations or states of the economy

- For one private good and two people, an *allocation* consists of *four* numbers (x_B, m_B, x_R, m_R), and *feasibility* requires $m_B + m_R + C(x_B + x_R) \leq \omega$.

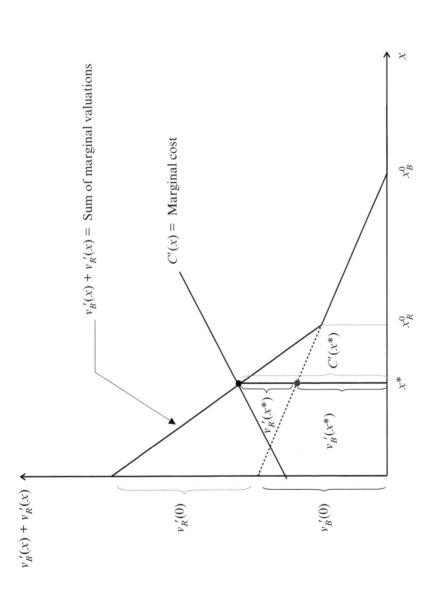

Figure 4.2 *The Samuelson condition with free disposal and high marginal cost*

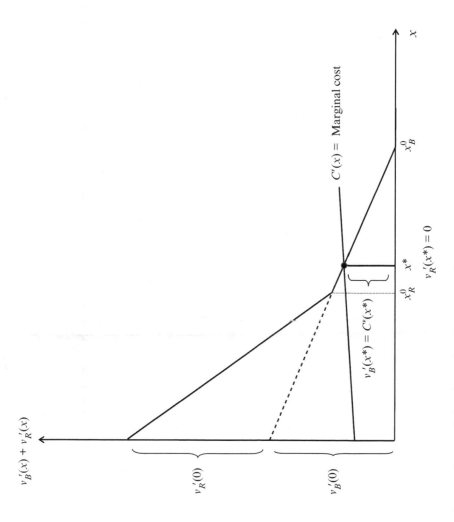

Figure 4.3 *The Samuelson condition with free disposal and low marginal cost*

- For one *public* good and two people, an *allocation* or *state of the economy* consists of *three* numbers (x, m_B, m_R), and *feasibility* requires $m_B + m_R + C(x) \leq \omega$.

Concept of economic efficiency
Same for both: a feasible allocation is *efficient* if there is no other feasible allocation (where feasibility is defined by the technology and resource constraints) that makes everybody better off.

Conditions for efficiency

1. No waste of numeraire (because if an allocation wastes numeraire, then we can find another allocation that is better for everybody; this is the condition of *production efficiency*)
   ○ In the case of a private good, this requires
     $m_B + m_R + C(x_B + x_R) = \omega$.
   ○ In the case of one public good, this requires $m_B + m_R + C(x) = \omega$.
2. Maximization of surplus (for quasilinear preferences; the argument is again that, otherwise, we can find another allocation that is better for everybody).

Marginal conditions for surplus maximization (under differentiability and positivity)

- In the case of a private good, surplus maximization requires the two equalities

$$v_B'(*x_B) = C'(x_B^* + x_R^*),$$
$$v_R'(*x_R) = C'(x_B^* + x_R^*),$$

as in (2.2) and (2.3) of Chapter 2.
- In the case of a public good, it requires the single equality (Samuelson condition)

$$v_B'(x^*) + v_R'(x^*) = C'(x^*).$$

Summarizing, at an efficient allocation involving a public good:

(a) *Everybody has available to him/her the same amount x* of the public good,* and:
(b) *The marginal valuation $v_i'(x^*)$ of different persons may be different, but:*
(c) *The sum of the marginal valuations equals the marginal cost.*

On the other hand, at an efficient allocation involving a private good not subject to externalities:

(a') *Everybody has the same marginal valuation, i.e.,* $v'_B(x^*_B) = v'_R(x^*_R)$;
(b') *The amount* x^*_i *consumed by different persons may be different,* but:
(c') *The sum of the amounts* x^*_i *consumed by different people must equal the amount produced, and the common marginal valuation must equal the marginal cost, i.e.,*

$$v'_B(x^*_B) = v'_R(x^*_R) = C'(^*x_B + x^*_R).$$

Graphically, in the case of public goods we depict the marginal condition for efficiency by equating the *vertically* added marginal valuation functions to the marginal cost, whereas in the private-good case we *horizontally* add the marginal valuation functions.

4.3   The provision of a public good through the political process

We consider three ways of allocating public goods.

* First, the political system, by far the most common institution for providing public goods.
* Second, voluntary contributions, a perhaps infrequent procedure which is nevertheless interesting because it illustrates the important *free rider* problem.
* Third, in the case of excludable public goods, a market-type scheme with user fees.

We begin with the pioneering contribution of Erik Lindahl.

4.3.1   Lindahl equilibrium

4.3.1.1   The simultaneous determination of provision and financing
Erik Lindahl (1891–1960), inspired by the ideas of his teacher Knut Wicksell (1851–1926), proposed a model of public good decision by a representative parliament.[7] His starting point was the observation that, because a public good should be made available to everybody, there should

---

[7] E. Lindahl (1919), "Positive Losung: der Gerechtigkeit der Besteurung," English translation in Richard A. Musgrave and Alan T. Peacock, editors, *Classics in the Theory of Finance*, London: MacMillan, 1958.

be some sort of unanimous agreement on its provision. In Wicksell's words:[8]

> Provided the expenditure in question holds out any prospect at all of creating utility exceeding costs, it will always be theoretically possible, and approximately so in practice, to find a distribution of costs such that all parties regard the expenditure as beneficial and may therefore approve it unanimously.

The Wicksell–Lindahl approach is based on two ideas. First, the principle of the *specialization of the budget*, i.e., the amount of the public good to be provided and the individual contributions towards covering its cost should be determined at the same time. Second, the *benefit principle*, i.e., the requirement that a person's contributions be in line with the benefit that she obtains from the public good. It should be noted that the benefit principle is opposed to the *ability-to-pay* or *equality of sacrifice* principle, according to which a wealthier person should contribute more that a poor one because equal contributions would force a greater sacrifice on the poor person. Wicksell and Lindahl defended the justice of benefit principle under the condition of a *just initial distribution of wealth*.

4.3.1.2 *Unanimity and the Lindahl equilibrium*

Lindahl considers a parliament where two parties, one representing the rich and one representing the poor, have to agree on how much of a public good to provide, and how to distribute its cost between the two groups.[9] Lindahl approaches the two questions as two sides of the same, two-dimensional issue, namely that of finding a share of the cost for each group that induces parties to propose the same quantity of the public good, so that the decision is unanimous.

Assume that, if they disagree, it is the smallest of the quantities proposed by rich and poor that is chosen. If the cost were equally distributed, then the poor would probably propose a smaller quantity of the public good. The rich would then be willing to shoulder a large cost share in order to induce the poor to accept a larger quantity of the good. A Lindahl equilibrium consists of two cost shares, one for the rich and one for the poor, that add up to one (100 percent) and that induce the two parties to propose the same quantity of the public good.

---

[8] K. Wicksell (1896), "Ein Neues Princip der gerechten Besteurung," English translation in Musgrave and Peacock, *op. cit.*, pp. 89–90.

[9] As Lindahl noted, the analysis can easily be extended to any number of political parties.

4.3.1.3 The Lindahl model

There are I_R rich persons with the same utility function, $U_R(x, m_i) = \sqrt{v_R(x)} + m_i$, where m_i is the consumption of numeraire by rich Person i, and the same initial wealth of ω_R units of numeraire.

Similarly, there are I_P poor people, each with utility function $U_P(x, m_h) = \sqrt{v_P(x)} + m_h$, where m_h is the consumption of numeraire by poor Person h, and the same initial wealth of ω_P units of numeraire.

The cost function is $C(x) = cx$, i.e., c is the constant average and marginal cost.

The parliament negotiates as follows. Somebody proposes that the rich pay the fraction s_R of the cost, and the poor s_P, where $s_R + s_P = 1$. The representatives of the rich then reply by announcing the quantity of the public good that maximizes the utility of their constituents, under the assumption that costs are equally shared within a group. Because a rich person ends up with $\omega_R - s_R cx/I_R$ units of numeraire after the corresponding contribution, she is interested in maximizing $v_R(x) + \omega_R - s_R cx/I_R$, where ω_R is a constant. Thus, the party representing the rich proposes the best level of x for the rich, given s_R, by solving the problem:

$$\text{given } s_R, \text{ choose the quantity } x \text{ that maximizes } -\frac{s_R cx}{I_R} + v_R(x).$$

Thus, the amount of the public good proposed by the party of the rich is defined (if positive) by the first-order condition

$$s_R = \frac{I_R v_R'(x)}{c}, \tag{4.5}$$

which condition is represented in Figure 4.4 as the solid curve in the coordinate system where the increasing direction on the vertical axis (with label s_R) is, as usual, upwards.

In a parallel manner, the representatives of the poor solve the maximization problem:

$$\text{given } s_P, \text{ choose the quantity } x \text{ that maximizes } -\frac{s_P cx}{I_P} + v_P(x),$$

with first order condition $s_P = I_P v_P'(x)/c$, which, because $s_P = 1 - s_R$, can be written

$$1 - s_R = \frac{I_P v_P'(x)}{c}. \tag{4.6}$$

Condition (4.6) is represented in Figure 4.4 as the dashed curve, where the variable s_P can be read off the downwards-pointing vertical axis. The Lindahl equilibrium is the point with coordinates x^* and s_R^*. The representative of the rich propose the quantity x^* given that they have to pay the

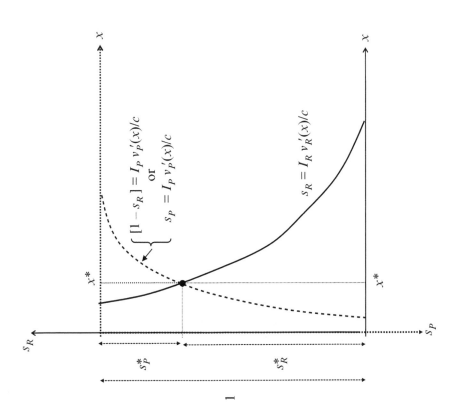

Figure 4.4 *Lindahl equilibrium*

fraction s_R^* of the cost, whereas the representative of the poor propose the same quantity x^* given that they have to pay the share $s_P^* = 1 - s_R^*$ of the cost. The decision is unanimous.

The Lindahl equilibrium agrees with the benefit principle in that the contribution of each person is proportional to the *marginal* (*not* the total) benefit that she derives from the public good. Indeed, we see from (4.5) that the contribution of a rich person is $s_R^* cx^*/I_R = v_R'(x^*)x^*$, which is the amount of the public good multiplied by a rich person's marginal valuation of it, whereas the contribution of a poor person is $v_P'(x^*)x^*$.

Lindahl believed that his model had both normative and positive relevance. Normatively, we will see in the following subsection that it satisfies economic efficiency. But its realism as a description of actual bargaining within the parliament of a representative democracy is debatable. Granted, often a consensus is sought, but the negotiation procedure proposed by Lindahl is by no means the only possible one. Second, the Lindahl procedure may be subject to manipulation (a feature that, we should recognize, is shared by many other systems), because the parties may understate the desired amount of the public good in order to end up with a lower cost share (s_R or s_P). Last but not least, few parliamentary negotiations follow the principle of the specialization of the budget, because the financing of public goods is often conditioned by existing tax laws that cannot be easily modified. But despite these difficulties, the Lindahl equilibrium remains a useful benchmark for both the positive and normative analysis of the allocation of public goods through the political process, in a role reminiscent of the one played by the competitive market equilibrium for private goods.

4.3.1.4   The efficiency of the Lindahl equilibrium

From (4.5) and (4.6) we have that

$$s_R^* c = I_R v_R'(x^*),$$

$$[1 - s_R^*]c = I_p v_p'(x^*).$$

Adding up and recalling that $C'(x) = c$, we obtain

$$I_R v_R'(x^*) + I_p v_p'(x^*) = c = C'(x^*),$$

which is precisely the Samuelson condition here.[10] Hence, the Lindahl equilibrium is efficient.

---

[10] In fact, it can be argued that Lindahl's (1919) analysis led to the Samuelson condition.

4.3.1.5 Social welfare at the Lindahl equilibrium

At the Lindahl equilibrium, the utility levels reached by a rich and a poor person are respectively

$$U_R\left(x^*, \omega_R - \frac{s_R^*}{I_R}cx^*\right) = \sqrt{v_R(x^*) + \omega_R - \frac{s_R^*}{I_R}cx^*},$$

$$U_P\left(x^*, \omega_P - \frac{s_P^*}{I_P}cx^*\right) = \sqrt{v_P(x^*) + \omega_P - \frac{s_P^*}{I_P}cx^*},$$

which in particular depend on the initial wealth levels ω_R and ω_P. As noted, Wicksell and Lindahl believed that the Lindahl equilibrium is just as long as the initial distribution of wealth is just. But the Lindahl equilibrium typically fails to maximize any given social welfare function. In particular, the resulting utility levels for rich and poor will be different, whereas the maximization of either the utilitarian or the maximin social welfare function requires equal utilities for our specification of the utility functions.[11]

4.3.2 The provision of a public good under an exogenous financing rule

4.3.2.1 Financing rules

As noted in Section 4.3.1.3 above, decisions by the public sector on public goods must often respect existing tax laws. We adopt this viewpoint for the remainder of Section 4.3: we postulate that the tax laws determine the tax or contribution of each person towards the financing of the public good. More precisely, we postulate a *tax rule*, i.e., I functions $t_i(x)$, $i = 1,\ldots, I$, one for each individual, interpreted as follows: $t_i(x)$ is the amount of numeraire that Person i will be taxed towards financing a supply x of the public good, $i = 1,\ldots, I$. We assume that $\Sigma_{i=1}^{I} t_i(x) = C(x)$, i.e., the exogenous financing rule exactly covers the cost of the public good.

Example 1. Head tax: $t_i(x) = C(x)/I$.

---

[11] The argument is that of Section 1.8.4 of Chapter 1 above: see also Section 3.3.5. The utilitarian maximization problem is here:

$$\max_{x,m_R} I_R\sqrt{v_R(x) + m_R} + I_P\sqrt{v_P(x) + \frac{\omega - C(x) - I_R m_R}{I_P}}.$$

The first-order equality for m_R is

$$I_R\frac{1}{2}[U_R]^{-1} + I_P\frac{1}{2}[U_P]^{-1}\cdot\left[-\frac{I_R}{I_P}\right] = 0,$$

which yields $U_R = U_P$. (The first-order equality for x then gives the Samuelson condition.)

Example 2. Linear income (or wealth) tax: $t_i(x) = [\omega_i/\Sigma_{h=1}^I \omega_h]C(x)$, where, for $h = 1,\ldots, I$, ω_h denotes the income or wealth of Person h.

Remark. Realistic income tax schedules are not linear but progressive. An affine tax approximates well actual income taxes.

Given a tax rule $t_i(x)$, $i = 1,\ldots, I$, we define Person i's *net benefit (or net valuation) function*

$$\beta_i(x) := v_i(x) - t_i(x).$$

4.3.2.2   Single-peaked net benefit functions

Person i's net benefit function $\beta_i(x)$ can, in principle, have any shape. Figures 4.5(a)–(d) show several possibilities. Figure 4.5(a) displays the net benefit of Person 1, who has a most preferred, or "peak" quantity $\hat{x}_1$ of the public good with the property, *if two alternative quantities x^1 and x^2 are located on the same side of $\hat{x}_1$, then the one closest to $\hat{x}_1$ is better for her*. We then say that Person 1's net benefit function is *single peaked*. Person 2's net benefit function, depicted in Figure 4.5(b), is also single peaked, with peak at $\hat{x}_2 = 0$.

But Person 3, represented in Figure 4.5(c), does not have a single-peaked net benefit function: x^3 is closer to x^1 than x^2, yet she prefers x^2 to x^3. Last, Figure 4.5(d) represents a net benefit function with ties. It is not single peaked, and we will rule it out, even though it could be shoehorned into the analysis at the cost of some complexity.

4.3.2.3   Median peaks and the Condorcet theorem

Let there be I persons, and assume that *each person has a single-peaked net benefit function*. Denote by $\hat{x}_i$ Person i's peak quantity of the public good. Let us look at the distribution of the numbers $\hat{x}_i$, some of which may appear more than once among our I consumers, and compute their *median* or "middle value," to be called the *median peak*, and denoted $\hat{x}_M$. If $\hat{x}_i = \hat{x}_M$, then we call Person i a *median voter, i.e., Person i is a median voter if her peak quantity, $\hat{x}_i$, is the median peak $\hat{x}_M$*.

Intuitively, we order people in a line according to their peak value, from smaller to larger (when two persons have the same peak, then their relative position in the line does not matter). If the number I of people is odd, there will be a middle position, with a person in it and with $[I - 1]/2$ persons on each side. This middle person is a median voter, and so are any persons with the same peak.

If the number I is even, then there may or may not be a median voter: the line is now divided into two halves, with nobody in the middle, and one person closest to the middle on each side of it. If the two persons closest to the middle have the same peak, then that peak is the median peak, and

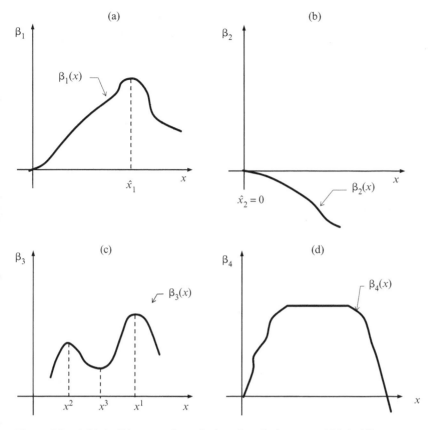

Figure 4.5   *4.5(a)–(b) are single-peaked net benefit functions 4.5(c)–(d) are not single-peaked net benefit functions*

those persons are median voters (as well as any other persons with the same peak). But if they have different peaks, then the median of the peaks is a number between the two peaks, which number is nobody's peak: no median voter then exists (say, if $I = 2$ and $\hat{x}_1 = 1$ and $\hat{x}_2 = 2$, then the median of the peaks is 1.5: this is nobody's peak, and no median voter exists).

The French mathematician and philosopher Marie Jean Antoine Nicolas Caritat, Marquis de Condorcet (1743–1794), pioneered the formal study of voting systems. The following theorem is inspired by his work. It is sometimes referred to as the "median voter theorem," although it should not be confused with the related Hotelling–Downs Median Voter Theorem discussed in the following section.

Condorcet Theorem for the case where there is a median voter. Let all persons have single-peaked net benefit functions. Consider a two-alternative vote (without abstention) between the median peak $\hat{x}_M$ and any other amount x of the public good. If a median voter exists, then $\hat{x}_M$ obtains more votes than x.

The proof is very simple. Without loss of generality, let $x < \hat{x}_M$. By the single-peak property, everybody with peak larger than (i.e., to the right of) $\hat{x}_M$ prefers $\hat{x}_M$ to x, and so does any median voter. If I is odd, then the number of voters to the right of the middle position, including that position is $1 + [I - 1]/2 = [I + 1]/2 > [I - 1]/2$, which is the number of people to the left (not including the middle). Thus, at least $[I + 1]/2$ vote for $\hat{x}_M$, and at most $[I - 1]/2$ vote for x.

If I is even, and a median voter exists, then the two persons closest to the middle must have the same peak $\hat{x}_M$. They and everybody to their right form a winning group of at least $I/2 + 1$, members, all voting for $\hat{x}_M$.

Define a *Condorcet winning alternative* (or a "Condorcet winner") as an amount x^* of the public good that, when paired in a two-alternative vote (without abstention) with any amount x of the public good, obtains at least as many votes as x. If there is a median voter, then the median peak is a Condorcet winning alternative. As seen in Section 4.3.2.3 above, no median voter exists if the number I is even and if the two persons closest to the middle have different peaks. A vote between these two peaks will result in a tie, but either of these two peaks will win a vote against any third alternative. Thus either of these two peaks is a Condorcet winning alternative. We then have the following theorem.

Condorcet Theorem for the general case where a median voter may or may not exist. Let all persons have single-peaked net benefit functions. Then there is a Condorcet winning alternative.

4.3.2.4 Multiple peaks and the Condorcet paradox

What if the net benefit function of one or more people fails to satisfy the condition of single peakedness? Surprising things may then happen, as illustrated by the *Condorcet*, or *voting*, *paradox*.

Postulate that a certain public good, say a park, can take only three values: small, medium and large (no park is not an option), denoted S, M and L. Let there be three persons ($I = 3$), named Alex, Gabriel and Eva. Their net benefit functions β_A, β_G, and β_E, respectively, are represented in Figure 4.6 as bar diagrams.

Alex is antipark: the smaller, the better; Gabriel is a moderate: he would prefer a medium size park, but if forced to choose between a large one and a small one, he would choose large. And Eva is an extremist: no middle of the road for her. She prefers large to small, and small to medium. What would be the results of pairwise voting?

- Between S and M: Alex and Eva vote for S; thus, S wins over M;
- Between S and L: Gabriel and Eva vote for L; thus, L wins over S;
- Between L and M: Alex and Gabriel vote for M; thus, M wins over L.

We first observe that *there is no Condorcet winning alternative*: M loses against S, S loses against L, and L loses against M.

Second, we note that, if there is in fact a sequence of pairwise votes, then a cycle occurs. For instance, M is defeated in the first pairwise vote listed above, but it reappears in the third vote and wins. In real-life politics, institutional design often prevents such cycles, but they may occasionally appear. Josephine Andrews argues that a sequence of votes in 1993 in the Russian parliament on the reform of the Russian constitution displayed such a cycle.[12] Various amendments were sequentially approved, but, at the end, the amended constitution was not approved. To put it in terms of the previous example, imagine that M is the old constitution, S is the old with one amendment, and L is the old with two amendments. First, one amendment passes as S wins over M. Then, the second amendment also passes as L wins over S. But then the so amended constitution loses against the unamended one, as L loses against M!

Third, we always assume that a rational consumer has transitive preferences. The Condorcet paradox evidences that if social preferences are defined by pairwise votes (i.e., society "prefers" x to y if x wins over y), then such preferences may be intransitive. In our example, S is "socially

---

[12] J.T. Andrews (2002), *When Majorities Fail: The Russian Parliament*, 1990–1993, Cambridge: Cambridge University Press. The finding is not uncontroversial: see Gerry Mackie (2003), *Democracy Defended*, Cambridge: Cambridge University Press.

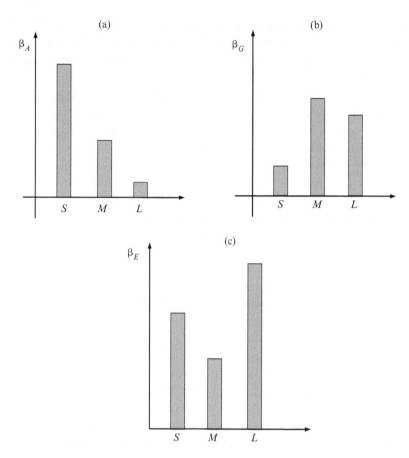

Figure 4.6   *The Condorcet paradox*

preferred" to M, and M is "socially preferred" to L. Transitivity would require S to be "socially preferred" to L, but here L is in fact "socially preferred" to M.[13]

Last, the Condorcet paradox illustrates the role of agenda setting when net benefit functions are not single peaked. Suppose, in our example, that the procedure for deciding among S, M and L is a two-step vote: first, two alternatives are paired, and the winning alternative is the paired against the remaining alternative.

If we first match S against M, then S wins, and is paired with L in the second step, and which point L wins. We end up with a large park. But, alternatively, suppose that the first vote is between S and L: then L wins the first round, but loses to M in the second round. A medium park is then chosen. Last, let the first vote be between M and L. Then M wins the first round, but loses to S in the second round, resulting in a small park.

Summarizing, the agenda determines the outcome. Whoever has the power to decide the voting order can in fact choose the outcome.

It should be emphasized that the paradox may only appear if some individual's net benefit function is not single peaked, because a Condorcet winning alternative must exist under single peakedness.[14] In particular, if there is a median voter, then her preferred alternative would be eventually chosen irrespective of the agenda.

4.3.2.5   One-dimensional political competition and the Hotelling–Downs median voter theorem

Harold Hotelling (1929, "Stability in competition," *Economic Journal*, 39(153), 41–57), Duncan Black (1948, "On the Rationale of Group Decision-making," *Journal of Political Economy*, 56, 23–34) and Anthony Downs (1957, *An Economic Theory of Democracy*, New York: Harper Collins) analyzed political competition between two non-ideological parties interested only in maximizing the probability of winning the election when there is a single policy issue, and, therefore, the political

---

[13] Arrow starts from this observation to develop his famous "impossibility theorem" (K.J. Arrow, 1951, *Social Choice and Individual Values*, New Haven, CT: Yale University Press).

[14] The condition needed for the Condorcet theorem is in fact that all individual net benefit functions be single peaked *for some common ordering of the alternatives on the horizontal axis*. Our Alex–Gabriel–Eva example violates this. In Figure 4.6(c), Eva is not single peaked and the order is S-M-L. We could make Eva single peaked by adopting the order M-L-S. But then Alex would not be single peaked. (The order S-M-L seems natural when interpreting these symbols as different sizes; but if, say, S stood for Swimming pool, M for Museum and L for Library, then S-M-L would be as natural as M-L-S.)

spectrum can be represented as a line.[15] The resulting model is often called the "median voter model" or the "spatial model of political competition."

Hotelling (1929) first developed a market model of product differentiation, which we may call the model of the *two ice-cream sellers on the beach.* Envision a linear beach, each location on it represented by a point in the interval [0, 1]. The model is formulated as a game between two ice-cream sellers, Seller 1 and Seller 2, who sell identical products at identical prices: a seller's only choice is her location on the beach: Seller 1 chooses her location σ_1 in the [0, 1] interval, and Seller 2 chooses hers, σ_2. They are both interested in maximizing sales. A large number of sunbathers are distributed along the length of the beach, and each of them will buy one, and only one, ice cream, and will go to the closest seller. If both sellers choose the same location, i.e., $\sigma_1 = \sigma_2$, then each gets one half of the market. But if they choose different locations, say $\sigma_1 < \sigma_2$, then Seller 1 gets every sunbather to her left, i.e., those in the subinterval [0, σ_1], plus those located between σ_1 and $[\sigma_2 - \sigma_1]/2$. (The sunbathers located exactly at $\sigma_1 + [\sigma_2 - \sigma_1]/2$ are indifferent between the two sellers: half of them go to each seller.) Hence, the set of possible strategies and the payoffs of the two players are well defined.

There is only one Cournot–Nash equilibrium of this game, where both sellers locate themselves in the median of the distribution of sunbathers. Note that this is indeed an equilibrium: if both you and your competitor are located at the median, then each of you is getting half of the market, whereas if you move away from it you will lose some of the customers between you and the other seller. Clearly, two different locations, say $\sigma_1 < \sigma_2$, cannot constitute an equilibrium, because any seller could then gain market by moving towards the other seller. And the same location for both, but away from the median, cannot be an equilibrium either, because each player is getting one half of the market, whereas by unilaterally moving towards the median she could get more than one half. Hence, the only equilibrium is $\tilde{\sigma}_1 = \tilde{\sigma}_2 = Median$, i.e., there is zero differentiation between the sellers.

Hotelling (1929) thought that he had discovered a general "principle of minimal differentiation" which could be applied to, say, religion and politics. In the political interpretation, the interval [0, 1] stands for, not a beach, but a one-dimensional political spectrum: say 0 is the "extreme left position," and 1 the "extreme right."[16] There are two parties, only

---

[15] Down's book was based on his Stanford Ph.D. thesis, written under the direction of Arrow, who, in turn, had been Hotelling's advisee (at Columbia).

[16] The Hotelling–Downs model is ill suited for the analysis of political competition with more than one issue or dimension, which requires a different approach. See J.E. Roemer (2001), *Political Competition*, Cambridge, MA: Harvard University Press.

interested in maximizing their vote share: Party i ($i = 1, 2$) chooses a position or platform σ_i in the [0, 1] spectrum. Voters have single-peaked preferences, and their peaks are distributed along this spectrum. Each voter votes (no abstention), choosing the party whose platform σ_i is closest to her own peak position. As in the beach model, at the unique Cournot–Nash equilibrium of the game each party proposes the policy preferred by the median voter and each gets 50 percent of the vote, winning the election with probability 50 percent.

The Hotelling–Downs view of the political process is quite dissimilar from that of Wicksell and Lindahl. Accordingly, their models are different, and so are the predicted outcomes. Table 4.1 highlights some differences.

4.3.2.6 Majority voting and economic efficiency

Assume that the financing rule is exogenously given, say, by previously approved tax laws, and that a decision is made by majority vote on the single issue of the quantity of the public good. Will the outcome be efficient?

The answer is "not necessarily." Consider a Yes–No public good. As noted in Section 4.2 above, efficiency requires that the good be provided if

$$\sum_{i=1}^{I} \overline{v}_i > \overline{C}, \tag{4.7}$$

and that it not be provided if

$$\sum_{i=1}^{I} \overline{v}_i < \overline{C}. \tag{4.8}$$

Suppose that, given the existing tax laws, Person i is taxed in the amount t_i if the public good is provided, with

$$\sum_{h=1}^{I} t_h = \overline{C}. \tag{4.9}$$

Then Person i's net benefit from the public good is

$$\beta_i := \overline{v}_i - t_i, \tag{4.10}$$

which can be positive or negative: in order to simplify the exposition, assume that it is not zero for any Person i.

Again postulate no abstention. If a vote is taken between Yes and No, what will Person i vote for? Clearly, she will vote Yes if $\beta_i > 0$, and No if $\beta_i < 0$. The outcome of the vote will be Yes if and only if the number of persons with positive β_i is larger than those with negative β_i. In other words, the outcome will be Yes if the median of the β_i' is

Table 4.1   *Political models: Wicksell–Lindahl vs. Hotelling–Downs*

	Wicksell–Lindahl	*Hotelling–Downs*
View of society	A few homogeneous social groups (say two, the rich and the poor)	A variety of heterogeneous individuals
Number of parties	As many as social groups	Two
Number of issues ("dimensionality of the policy space")	Several issues (in the case of one public good, both x and s_P are decided; moreover, the analysis can easily be extended to many public goods. Thus, the policy space is multidimensional)	Only one issue (only one public good can be considered, and the financing rule is exogenous; thus, only x is decided. The policy space is unidimensional)
Modus operandi	Parties negotiate in the parliament	Parties compete for votes with electoral platforms (each party proposes an amount of the public good)
Objective of parties	The welfare of their constituents (parties are *representative*)	To win the election (parties are *Downsian*)
Outcome	An efficient state of the economy	$x = \hat{x}_M$ (the median peak), with financing determined by the exogenous rule, often yielding an inefficient state

positive, and No if the median is negative. This agrees with the median voter analysis of the previous section, because with only two alternatives, and assuming that β_i is different from zero, all net benefit functions are trivially single peaked.

Is the outcome of the vote efficient? It depends. By (4.7), (4.9) and (4.10), efficiency requires that the good be provided if $\Sigma_{i=1}^{I}\beta_i > 0$, i.e., if the *mean* of the β_i' is positive, and, by (4.8), that it not be provided if the mean is negative. Thus, the outcome of the vote is efficient if the median and the mean are either both positive or both negative. But the outcome is inefficient if one is positive and the other one is negative. For example, let $I = 5$, with $\beta_1 = -3, \beta_2 = -2, \beta_3 = -1, \beta_4 = 6$ and $\beta_5 = 10$. The median voter is Person 3, with a negative net valuation: hence the voting outcome is No. But the mean net valuation is $[-6 + 16]/5 = 2 > 0$. Hence, efficiency requires Yes, and the voting outcome is inefficient.

In a sense, the inefficiency is caused by the lack of flexibility in the financing of the public good, contrary to what happened at the Lindahl equilibrium. Because the tax rule is fixed, there is no room for a political compromise that could yield a win–win outcome. Nevertheless, Donald Wittman has argued that, in the actual operation of political systems, participants often find a way to reach efficient outcomes.[17]

4.4   The provision of a public good by voluntary contributions

4.4.1   *The voluntary contribution game*

Public goods might be provided by *voluntary contributions*. Consider a neighborhood that wishes to have fireworks on the Fourth of July. Each neighbor contributes a certain amount of numeraire to a pot, and the size of the fireworks is what can be supplied with the sum of the contributions. We ask: how is the quantity of the public good (size of fireworks) determined? Is it efficient?

We maintain the hypothesis that the consumer only cares about the amount of the public good provided and about her contribution. In particular, she does not directly care about the contributions by other people: only on their effect on the amount of the public good available. This formulation does not cover preferences on the relative contributions of various people, such as feelings of being unfairly exploited if other people contribute relatively little, or of lack of solidarity. These considerations may well play a role in real-life voluntary contributions or in laboratory

[17] D. Wittman (1995), *The Myth of Democratic Failure: Why Political Institutions are Efficient*, Chicago: University of Chicago Press.

experiments, but will be ignored here. The main lesson of the model is the presence of incentives to *free ride*.

The idea can be formalized as a game: see Appendix 1B above. Let there be I players, and let the amount x of the public good be a continuous, nonnegative variable. We maintain quasilinearity, with i's valuation function $v_i(x)$, i.e., i's utility function is, as usual, $U_i(x, m_i) = \sqrt{v_i(x)} + m_i$. We postulate that the marginal valuation functions v_i' are decreasing as long as their values are positive.[18] Player i is initially endowed with ω_i units of numeraire. We assume that $C(x) = x$: one unit of numeraire yields exactly one unit of the public good.

Player i decides on her *contribution* t_i of numeraire towards the supply of the public good. *We require t_i to be nonnegative.* (You can contribute to the pot, but you *cannot* withdraw from it.) If the contributions of the I persons are $(t_1, \ldots, t_I)$, then the amount of public good supplied is $\sum_{h=1}^{I} t_h$, and player i attains the utility level $\sqrt{v_i(\sum_{h=1}^{I} t_h)} + \omega_i - t_i$.

4.4.2   Equilibrium contributions

In game-theoretic terms, a nonnegative number t_i is a possible *strategy* of player i. The *payoff* to i can be understood to be her utility, or, more simply, her net benefit $v_i(\sum_{h=1}^{I} t_h) - t_i$, a function of the strategy tuple $(t_1, \ldots, t_I)$. A Cournot–Nash equilibrium of the voluntary contribution game is a tuple $(\tilde{t}_1, \ldots, \tilde{t}_I)$ of strategies (i.e., contributions) such that, for Player i ($i = 1, \ldots, I$), $\tilde{t}_i$ maximizes

$$v_i\left(t_i + \sum_{\substack{h=1 \\ h \neq i}}^{I} \tilde{t}_h\right) - t_i \tag{4.11}$$

subject to the condition that t_i cannot be negative, a condition that plays an important role because she may decide to contribute nothing. In other words, $\tilde{t}_i$ is Player i's *best reply* to the other players' strategies $\tilde{t}_h$, $h \neq i$.

At the solution to Player i's maximization problem, either she contributes an amount for which the marginal net benefit that she derives from her contribution is zero, or she sets $t_i = 0$, contributing nothing, in which case the marginal net benefit cannot be positive, i.e., from (4.11),

$$either\ t_i > 0,\ and\ v_i'\left(t_i + \sum_{\substack{h=1 \\ h \neq i}}^{I} t_h\right) = 1, \tag{4.12}$$

---

[18] We also assume that the limit, as x tends to infinity, of $v_i'(x)$ is less than one, to rule out uninteresting situations.

$$or\ t_i = 0,\ and\ v_i'\left(t_i + \sum_{\substack{h=1 \\ h \neq i}}^{I} t_h \right) \leq 1. \tag{4.13}$$

In order to find the Cournot–Nash equilibrium or equilibria, we first focus on Player i and ask: what would be Player i's contribution if she were the only person who contributes? Call it i's *stand-alone contribution*, and denote it $\hat{t}_i$. In other words, $\hat{t}_i$ maximizes $v_i(t_i) - t_i$, which coincides with (4.11) when

$$\sum_{\substack{h=1 \\ h \neq i}}^{I} \tilde{t}_h = 0.$$

The conditions imposed above on marginal valuation functions guarantee that either $v_i'(0) < 1$, or that there is a unique, positive solution to the equation $v_i'(t_i) = 1$. Hence $\hat{t}_i$ satisfies

$$either\ \hat{t}_i > 0\ and\ v_i'(\hat{t}_i) = 1, \tag{4.14}$$

$$or\ \hat{t}_i = 0\ and\ v_i'(0) \leq 1. \tag{4.15}$$

The case of (4.14) is illustrated in Figure 4.7 and that of (4.15) in Figure 4.8. Note that, in either case, $\hat{t}_i$ would be Player i's best reply to everybody else contributing nothing. In (4.14) and Figure 4.7, Player i's best reply varies with the amount of contributions by the others. If the others contribute nothing, then Player i's best reply is indeed to contribute $\hat{t}_i$, but if the others contribute a positive amount, then Player i's best reply is to contribute *less than* $\hat{t}_i$, may be even zero. Indeed, let the sum of contributions by the others be

$$\sum_{\substack{h=1 \\ h \neq i}}^{I} t_h := t^0 < \hat{t}_i,$$

as in Figure 4.7. Then Player i's best reply is to contribute $\hat{t}_i - t^0$, so equating the marginal value to her, $v_i'(t_i + t^0)$, of her contribution to its marginal cost to her, -1, as in (4.12). But if the sum of contributions by the others is $t^1 \geq \hat{t}_i$, as in Figure 4.7, then Player i's best reply is to contribute nothing (recall that i cannot contribute negative amounts), in accordance with (4.13).

This argument leads to the following algorithm to find the Cournot–Nash equilibrium, or equilibria, of the voluntary contribution game.

STEP 1. Find the stand-alone contribution of each player, i.e., compute $\hat{t}_i$ for $i = 1,\ldots, I$.

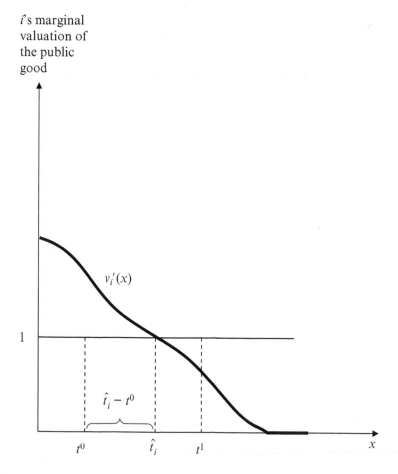

Figure 4.7   *Player i's stand-alone contribution is positive*

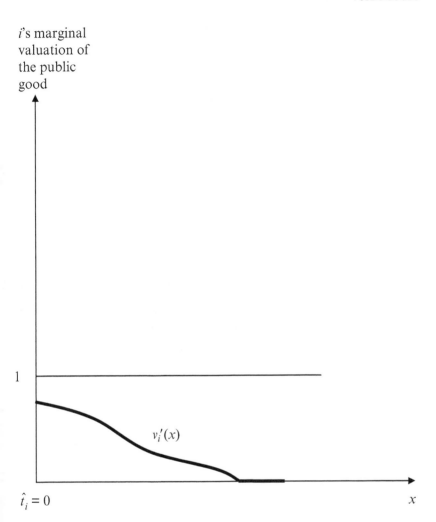

Figure 4.8   *Player i's stand-alone contribution is zero*

STEP 2. Find the player or players (the "top valuators") with the largest stand-alone contribution, and define $\hat{t}$ as the largest of the $\hat{t}_i$', i.e., $\hat{t} \geq \hat{t}_i$, for every player i.

STEP 3. The level of the public good provided at any Cournot–Nash equilibrium equals the largest stand-alone contribution, $\hat{t}$, i.e., that of a top valuator, and players who are not top valuators contribute nothing, hence "free riding" on whoever contributes. Moreover

1. *If there is only one top valuator, then at equilibrium she contributes $\hat{t}$.*
2. *If there are several top valuators, then any contributions by the top valuators that add up to $\hat{t}$ constitute an equilibrium.*

We may argue detail as follows. There may in principle be several top valuators, but consider first the case where there is only one, say Player 1, i.e., $\hat{t} = \hat{t}_1 > \hat{t}_i$, for all $i \neq 1$. If Player 1 contributes $\hat{t}$, then (as illustrated by t^1 in Figure 4.7) everybody else's best reply is to contribute nothing. And if everybody but Player 1 contributes nothing, then Player 1's best reply is to contribute $\hat{t}_1$ (by the definition of her stand-alone contribution). Thus the tuple of contributions $(\hat{t}_1, 0,\ldots, 0)$ is a Cournot–Nash equilibrium, everybody else "free rides" on Player 1.[19]

Alternatively, let there be several top valuators, say players 1, 2,..., I_C, all with stand-alone contribution $\hat{t} := \hat{t}_1 = \hat{t}_2 = \ldots = \hat{t}_{I_C} > \hat{t}_i$, for all $i > I_C$ (perhaps $I_C = I$, which will occur if all players have the same valuation function). Then *any distribution of the amount $\hat{t}$ among 1, 2,..., I_C, with zero contribution by everybody else* (i.e., any vector of contributions of the form $(t_1, t_2, \ldots, t_{I_C}, 0, \ldots, 0)$ with $\Sigma_{i=1}^{I_C} t_i = \hat{t}$) *is a Cournot–Nash equilibrium.* Indeed, as long as the aggregate contribution is $\hat{t}$, only players 1 to I_C may have positive contributions at equilibrium: (4.12) is satisfied by any Player i with positive contributions and (4.13) is satisfied by anybody else. Thus, the amount of the public good provided is $\hat{t}$, and players with $\hat{t}_i < \hat{t}$ contribute nothing, as before. But now there is a degree of indeterminacy in the allocation of $\hat{t}$ among top valuators.

4.4.3   The inefficiency of the voluntary contributions equilibrium

Typically, the level of the public good at any Cournot–Nash equilibrium is inefficiently low. Note that $\hat{t}$ equates the marginal cost to the marginal valuation of *one* player (namely a top valuator), whereas efficiency requires the marginal cost to equal the *sum* of the marginal valuations of all players. There may be exceptional situations when the outcome is efficient. For instance, if there is a unique top valuator, and everybody

---

[19] One can easily show that this is the only equilibrium.

else's marginal valuation of the public good at $\hat{t}$ is zero, then the marginal valuation of the top valuator at $\hat{t}$ is the sum of the marginal valuations. Efficient equilibria may also be present if the public good can only take two values, $x = 0$ and $x = 1$. But, typically, the equilibrium outcome is inefficient.

4.4.4 Many identical players

Suppose now that we have I players with identical valuation functions, namely

$$v_i(x) = ax - 0.5 \, bx^2, \, i = 1, \ldots, I,$$

Efficiency requires satisfying the Samuelson condition "$I[a - b \, x] = 1$," i.e.,

$$x^* = \frac{1}{b}\left[a - \frac{1}{I}\right],$$

as long as that this expression is nonnegative, otherwise the efficient amount of the public good is zero. But this expression is positive for large I, even if $a < 1$. Assume that this is the case, i.e., $a > 1/I$.

Everybody is a top valuator here, with the common stand-alone contribution

$$\hat{t} = \begin{cases} \dfrac{a - 1}{b}, \text{if } a > 1, \\ 0, \text{if } a \le 1, \end{cases}$$

an amount that, even when positive, is less than the efficient quantity (as long as $I > 1$). Thus, the equilibrium amount of the public good is inefficiently low.

Let contributions be positive and symmetric, i.e., everybody contributes $\hat{t}/I = [a - 1]/Ib$. Would you say that a player "free rides"? If you say No, then you admit that there can be inefficiency without free riding.

4.5 The provision of an excludable public good by charging user fees

4.5.1 Efficient pricing

If exclusion is possible and not too costly, then a public or private firm can in principle supply a public good or service and charge user fees. Because we are dealing with nonrival goods, we will refer to amounts *made available to* the consumer, or *accessed by* the consumer, rather than "consumed," which term suggests the destruction of the "consumed" object.

What prices or user fees would yield economic efficiency? We already observed that, even though it is now possible to make different amounts available to different people, for the purposes of analyzing efficiency there is no loss of generality in assuming that the same amount is made available to everybody, because it would be inefficient to restrict the access of a person with positive marginal valuation. Thus, the problem of efficient pricing can be discussed, under quasilinearity, in two steps. First, determine the amount x^* of the public good consistent with efficiency. Second, characterize the pricing schemes that induce all users to demand the amount x^*. We now show that efficient price may require "personalized" prices, i.e., different prices or access fees are charged to different people.

4.5.2 Lindahl prices for a continuous public good

Consider first a public good that is a continuous variable. Postulate the following two assumptions. First, what a consumer pays per unit of the public good accessed does not depend on how many units she accesses. We call this *linear* pricing: if, say, Consumer i is charged p_i (units of numeraire) per unit of the public good accessed, and she accesses x_i units, then she pays $p_i x_i$. Second, assume that *no consumer is rationed*, i.e., if at price p_i she wants to access x_i units, then x_i units are made available to her.

Efficient pricing then requires charging personalized prices formally similar to the cost shares for the rich and for the poor in the Lindahl equilibrium.[20] Indeed, let there be I people, with valuation functions $v_i(x)$ for $i = 1,\ldots, I$, and, as usual, let $C(x)$ be the cost of providing the good or service, so that social surplus is $S(x) := \Sigma_{i=1}^{I} v_i(x) - C(x)$. Let $x^* > 0$ maximize social surplus, which (under differentiability) implies the Samuelson condition

$$\sum_{i=1}^{I} v_i'(x^*) = C'(x^*).$$

Efficiency then requires charging Person i a price p_i per unit of the good or service that induces her to choose the level x^*. Because her demand is given by the *Price = Marginal valuation* condition $p_i = v_i'(x)$, Person i should be charged her marginal valuation at x^*, i.e.,

$$p_i = v_i'(x^*). \tag{4.16}$$

---

[20] In fact, Duncan Foley (1970, "Lindahl's solution and the core of an economy with public goods," *Econometrica*, 38, 66–72) proposed a by now popular interpretation of a Lindahl equilibrium in terms of a market with personalized prices, instead of the political party negotiation originally presented by Lindahl (1919).

A price p_i *higher* than $v_i'(x^*)$ would lead Person i to access a quantity of the public good lower than x^*, which is inefficient. A price p_i *lower* than $v_i'(x^*)$ would lead to the rationing of her demand when only x^* units of the public good are provided.

Figure 4.9 reproduces the information of Figures 4.2 and 4.1 above and illustrates the case where, at x^*, both marginal valuations are positive. At the prices of (4.16), both Blue and Red demand to access the efficient amount x^* of the public good.

But, depending on the magnitude of marginal costs relative to the marginal valuations, it may occur that, at x^*, the marginal valuations of some consumers are zero. Efficient pricing then requires letting them access the public good without charge. Figure 4.10 (with the data of Figure 4.3) illustrates: Red's marginal valuation at x^* is zero, and he is charged nothing.[21]

If prices are personalized in accordance with (4.16), then the revenue of the firm or entity that provides the public good is, using the Samuelson condition,

$$x^* \sum_{i=1}^{I} p_i = x^* \sum_{i=1}^{I} v_i'(x^*) = x^* C'(x^*).$$

In words, revenue would cover costs only if average costs were not lower than marginal costs. But often economies of scale are present in the production of public goods, in which case marginal costs are lower than average costs, and a firm practicing this type of pricing would suffer losses. Chapter 5 below considers this issue.

4.5.3   Access fees for a Yes–No public good

Alternatively, consider a Yes–No public good or service. As noted in Section 4.2.2 above, efficiency requires that the service be provided if

$$\sum_{i=1}^{I} \bar{v}_i > \bar{C}. \tag{4.17}$$

Assume that this is the case. If the good is provided through a market, then each person should face an access fee A_i low enough so as not to discourage her from accessing the public good. Hence, fees should satisfy the *participation constraint*

$$A_i \le \bar{v}_i. \tag{4.18}$$

Fees will exactly cover costs if

---

[21] Does Red free ride? If you say Yes, then you admit that there may be free riding without inefficiency: compare with the last sentence in Section 4.4.4 above.

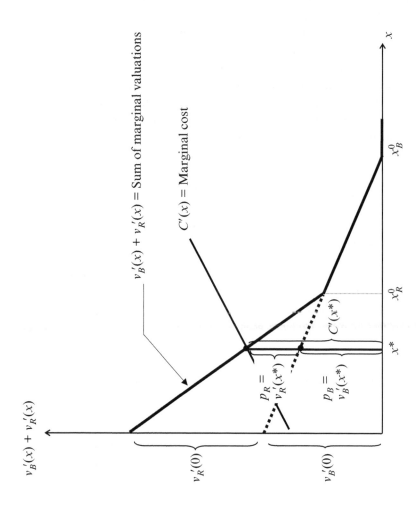

Figure 4.9 *The Samuelson condition and Lindahl prices when all marginal valuations are positive at x**

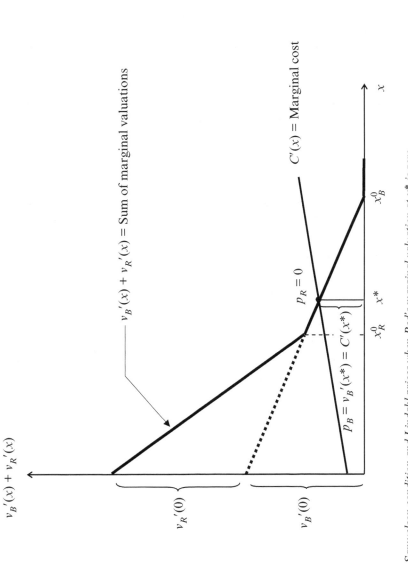

Figure 4.10 *The Samuelson condition and Lindahl prices when Red's marginal valuation at x* is zero*

$$\sum_{i=1}^{I} A_i = \overline{C}. \tag{4.19}$$

Of course, (4.17) guarantees that fees satisfying (4.18)–(4.19) can be found. But if the values $\overline{v}_i$ vary across individuals, then (4.18)–(4.19) may require different fees. If, say, $I = 2$, $\overline{C} = 3$, $\overline{v}_B = 3.5$ and $\overline{v}_R = 1$, then (4.18) requires that $A_R \leq 1$, and hence $A_B \geq 2$. This is illustrated in Figure 4.11(a). The combinations (A_B, A_R) of access fees that satisfy (4.18) are those in the shaded rectangle, whereas those that satisfy (4.19) are the ones on the line through $(\overline{C}, 0)$ and $(0, \overline{C})$. The solid segment depicts those combinations that satisfy both (4.18) and (4.19), which in Figure 4.11(a) does not intersect the 45° line. Hence, personalized access fees are required for efficiency. But if the valuations are not too different, as in Figure 4.11(b), then an equal division of the cost satisfies both (4.18) and (4.19), i.e., the access fee can be made uniform.

If efficiency requires personalized access fees, we may ask the second-best question: how can surplus be maximized subject to the condition that the supplier breaks even and access fees are uniform? Let there be I consumers, with valuations $\overline{v}_i$, $i = 1, \ldots, I$. The second-best uniform access fee A must maximize the number $\overline{I}$ of consumers for whom $\overline{v}_i \geq A$ subject to $\overline{I}A \geq \overline{C}$. If there are only two consumers, Blue and Red, with $\overline{v}_R < \overline{C}/2$ and $\overline{v}_B \geq \overline{C}$ (modify Figure 4.11(a) by increasing $\overline{v}_B$ so that $\overline{v}_B \geq \overline{C}$), then the second-best solution sets $A \geq \overline{C}$, with only Blue accessing. But if the data are as in Figure 4.11(a), then the second-best solution entails not supplying the good at all.

We will revisit some of these issues in Chapter 5 below, on public utility pricing and natural monopoly, and show that some features of markets for excludable public goods display an appealing parallelism there.

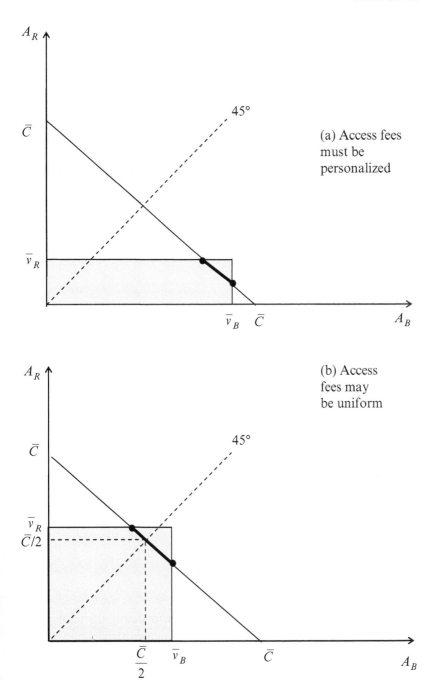

Figure 4.11   *Access fees for an excludable, Yes–No public good*

Appendix 4A   Public goods in the continuum economy

Let X be a Yes–No public good or project, say, the preservation of an endangered species where "zero" is interpreted as "extinction," and "one" as "preservation" (see Section 1.8.2 above). Assume that once the public good is supplied, it is made available to everybody. Denote by $\overline{C}$ the cost of supplying the public good. (As usual, we postulate that the cost of not supplying the public good is zero.)

As in Section 1A.1 above, a function $m(n)$ indicates the consumption of the numeraire good by each consumer $n \in (0, N_0]$. Allocating the numeraire according to $m(n)$ while supplying the public good is feasible if

$$\int_0^{N_0} m(n)\,dn + \overline{C} \le \omega,$$

whereas if the public good is not supplied, then the feasibility condition is

$$\int_0^{N_0} m(n)\,dn \le \omega,$$

compare with (1.3) above. By substituting equality signs for the weak inequality signs in the two previous expressions we obtain the production efficiency condition.

In a manner parallel to 1A.2 above, let $\overline{v}(n)$ denote the valuation of the public good by person n. The surplus function can take only two values, zero (the social surplus of not supplying the public good is zero), and $\overline{S}$, interpreted as the surplus achieved by supplying the public good and given by

$$\overline{S} := \int_0^{N_0} \overline{v}(n)\,dn - \overline{C},$$

compare with (1.7) above. Efficiency requires to supply the public good if $\overline{S} > 0$, and not to supply it if $\overline{S} < 0$, in a manner parallel to condition (4.17) found in section 4.5.3 above for the case where the number of consumers is finite.

We now consider the case where the public good is excludable, so that user fees can be charged. As in Section 4.5.3 above, we ask: when $\overline{S} > 0$, can efficiency be achieved while user fees cover the cost $\overline{C}$? The answer, as in there, is Yes if personalized fees are allowed. For instance, n can be charged an access fee of $A(n) = t\overline{v}(n)$, where

$$t = \frac{\overline{C}}{\displaystyle\int_0^{N_0} \overline{v}(n)\,dn} < 1,$$

resulting in an aggregate fee of

$$\int_0^{N_0} A(n)\,dn = t \int_0^{N_0} \overline{v}(n)\,dn = \frac{\overline{C}}{\displaystyle\int_0^{N_0} \overline{v}(n)\,dn} \int_0^{N_0} \overline{v}(n)\,dn = \overline{C}.$$

But if fees have to be uniform, then it depends on how different people are: positive fees may discourage people with small but positive $\overline{v}(n)$, resulting in inefficiency. In that case, we may consider, as in Section 4.5.3 above (and as in Section 5.3.3 and Appendix 5A below), the second-best problem of maximizing social surplus subject to covering the cost by means of a uniform access fee. As in there, depending on the data the second-best solution may entail supplying the public good to an inefficiently low number of users, or not supplying it at all. To illustrate the last case, let $\overline{v}(n) = N_0 - n$ and $\overline{C} = [N_0]^2/3 > 0$. First note that

$$\overline{S} = \int_0^{N_0} [N_0 - n]\,dn - \overline{C} = N_0 \int_0^{N_0} dn - \int_0^{N_0} n\,dn - \frac{[N_0]^2}{3}$$

$$= [N_0]^2 - \frac{1}{2}[N_0]^2 - \frac{[N_0]^2}{3} = \frac{[N_0]^2}{6} > 0.$$

Hence, efficiency requires the provision of the public good. But the supplier of the public good can never break even with a uniform access fee. Revenue as a function of N is given by $[N_0 - N]N$, maximized when $N_0 - 2N = 0$ and hence when the access fee is $A = N_0 - N_0/2$. But this yields a maximal revenue of just $[N_0]^2/4$, insufficient to cover the cost of $[N_0]^2/3$. Hence, no uniform access fee can generate enough revenue to cover the cost.

5 Public utilities

. . . .

5.1 Capacity costs and operating costs

We return to the private good, no externality, quasilinear economy of Section 2.1 in Chapter 2, with two consumers, Ms. Blue and Mr. Red, with utility functions:

$$\text{Blue: } U_B(x_B, m_B) = \sqrt{v_B(x_B)} + m_B, \text{ with } v_B(0) = 0,$$

$$\text{Red: } U_R(x_R, m_R) = \sqrt{v_R(x_R)} + m_R, \text{ with } v_R(0) = 0,$$

where we explicitly assume free disposal, i.e.,

$$v_i'(x_i) \geq 0, i = B, R. \tag{5.1}$$

But we postulate that the cost of providing x_B units of good X to Blue and x_R units of good X to Red can be decomposed into a capacity cost and operating costs, i.e.,

Total cost = Capacity cost + Operating costs.

Operating costs are separable: the operating cost for the production of x_B (resp. x_R) depends only on x_B (resp. x_R), and we assume, for simplicity, that it is proportional to x_B (resp. x_R): hence, average operating costs are constant and equal to marginal operating costs.

But the capacity cost is a joint cost: we interpret capacity as an input whose use in the production of x_B is nonrival with its use in the production of x_R. Hence, capacity has the character of a public good in production. For this reason, even though good X is rival in consumption, and hence a private good, the analysis of its efficient pricing displays an appealing parallelism with the pricing of excludable public goods just discussed in Section 4.5 of Chapter 4 above.

We frequently observe technologies fitting this description in the provision of private goods such as energy, communication and transportation. The firms providing these goods, publicly owned or regulated, are often referred to as public utilities.

Capacity may be a continuous variable, or a Yes–No variable. We first (Section 5.2 below), assume that capacity is continuous: the pricing of capacity is then formally similar to the Lindahl pricing of a continuous public good analysed in Section 4.5.2. We study *peak-load* pricing in this model.

Capacity is a Yes–No variable in Section 5.3 below: "No" implies that no output can be produced, whereas "Yes" means that any amount of output can be produced by incurring the corresponding operating cost. We use this second model to analyse *natural monopolies*, showing that the efficient pricing of natural-monopoly goods is parallel to that of a Yes–No, or "dichotomous," public good explored in Section 4.5.3.

5.2   Capacity as a continuous variable and peak-load pricing

5.2.1   Costs

A typical public utility offers a variety of services that are often subject to the same capacity constraint, such as daytime vs. nighttime or summer vs. winter demand for electricity. Instances of time-dependent demand are also common in travel (subways and bridges at peak vs. off-peak periods) and communications (telephones at midmorning vs. midnight).

We may interpret good X as electricity, Blue's consumption (x_B) occurring at peak-time and Red's (x_R) off-peak. A cost function of the form $c[x_B + x_R]$ would be inappropriate: to supply 25 during the day and 5 at night will typically cost more than to supply 15 during both day and night, since a large component of the cost is directly related to the size of the power plant. In order to supply 25 during the day and 5 at night, a large power plant is needed (underutilized at night), whereas in order to supply 15 and 15 a substantially smaller power plant will suffice.

The capacity cost, an important component of the total cost in power generation, as it is in telecommunications and transportation, is interpreted as the cost of building a plant or facility able to supply the amounts x_B and x_R. We postulate that a plant of any size or capacity k can be built, and hence capacity is a continuous variable. The amounts of good X supplied, x_B and x_R, are bounded by the capacity available. Measuring capacity k in the same units as good X, we must then have

$$x_B \leq k,$$

$$x_R \leq k,$$

i.e., the size of the plant needed to supply (x_B, x_R) must be no less than the maximum of the two numbers x_B and x_R. Let us ignore the complications caused by uncertainty, e.g., the need for slack in capacity to cover random surges in demand, certainly significant in the real-life supply of electricity. If we assume that demand is known with certainty, then a plant larger than the maximum of the two numbers x_B and x_R is wasteful. Accordingly, the capacity needed to supply (x_B, x_R) is $k = \max\{x_B, x_R\}$.

We take the capacity cost to be proportional to capacity k, i.e., φk. The cost function is then:

$$\tilde{C}(x_B, x_R) = \varphi \max\{x_B, x_R\} + c_B x_B + c_R x_R,$$

where:

φ is the marginal capacity cost (equal to the capacity cost per unit of capacity);

c_B is the peak-time (Blue) marginal operating cost, equal to the per unit operating cost of peak-time supply (may be interpreted as fuel cost);

c_R is the off-peak (Red) marginal operating cost (equal to the per unit operating cost of off-peak-time supply).[1]

5.2.2 Peak-load pricing under zero operating costs

Envision that Blue or Red can access a plant of capacity k to produce any amounts $x_B \leq k$ and $x_R \leq k$, respectively, without depleting or reducing the existing capacity. They do that at different times: Blue during the peak period and Red off-peak, so that they do not interfere with each other. This gives capacity a public good character. The efficient pricing of capacity then becomes a form of Lindahl pricing discussed in Section 4.5.2. Note that there is "free disposal" of capacity: in particular, Red is free not to fully use the capacity k.

A consumer direct valuation of good X (electricity, say), which enters her or his utility functions, induces an indirect valuation of capacity, a means for producing good X. We shall notationally distinguish between a consumer's marginal valuation of good X and her or his marginal valuation of capacity.

To develop the intuition, consider first the extreme case $c_B = c_R = 0$, i.e., zero operating costs. In that case, the marginal valuations of good X coincide with those of capacity, i.e., denoting the *marginal valuation of capacity* by $\hat{v}_i'(k)$, for $i = B, R$:

$$\textit{Marginal valuation of } k \textit{ units of capacity} := \hat{v}_i'(k)$$
$$= v_i'(k) := \textit{Marginal valuation of } k \textit{ units of good } X.$$

---

[1] This technology presents *constant returns to scale*. Economies of scale can be introduced adding a fixed cost F, as in Section 5.3 below.

By (5.1), $v_i'(k) \geq 0$, and hence the equality "$\hat{v}_i'(k) = v_i'(k)$" can be written

$$\hat{v}_i'(k) = \max\{v_i'(k), 0\}, \, i = B, R. \tag{5.2}$$

We can now apply the analysis of Section 4.5.2 of Chapter 4 above to the public good k with marginal valuation functions $\hat{v}_B'(k)$ and $\hat{v}_R'(k)$. First, we compute the efficient level k^* of capacity by solving the Samuelson condition

$$\hat{v}_B'(k) + \hat{v}_R'(k) = \varphi, \tag{5.3}$$

and then we charge the Lindahl prices for capacity:

Blue: $\varphi_B = \hat{v}_B'(k^*)$ per unit of capacity that she accesses, (5.4)

Red: $\varphi_R = \hat{v}_R'(k^*)$ per unit of capacity that he accesses. (5.5)

Again by the Samuelson condition, $\varphi_B + \varphi_R = \varphi$.
As in Section 4.5.2, two cases may occur.[2]

Case 1. Red's marginal valuation of capacity at k^* is zero, as occurred with Red in Figure 4.10 of Chapter 4. Then Red does not fully use capacity (i.e., $x_R^* < k^*$), and does not pay for it. The personalized prices for capacity are:

Blue: $\varphi_B = \varphi,$ (5.6)

Red: $\varphi_R = 0.$ (5.7)

This is the typical situation in peak-load pricing.

Case 2. Alternatively, both Blue and Red may fully use capacity, as in Figure 4.9 of Chapter 4; then both are charged the positive prices for capacity given by (5.4) and (5.5).
There are no other charges when $c_B = c_R = 0$.

5.2.3 Peak-load pricing under positive operating costs

The idea can be extended to the case where c_B and c_R are positive. A capacity of k kW permits the production of $x_i \leq k$ kW of electricity for

---

[2] We assume that peak-time demand is not lower than off-peak demand, i.e., $x_B \geq x_R$.

Consumer i at a unit operating cost of c_i. Efficiency then requires that the price p_i of good X (electricity) charged to Consumer i ($i = B, R$) be the sum of her (or his) Lindahl price for capacity, φ_i, and her marginal operating cost, i.e.,

$$p_i = \varphi_i + c_i, i = B, R. \tag{5.8}$$

To find Consumer i's marginal valuation of capacity, imagine that she (or he) takes care of her own operating cost (fuel, say), and accesses the plant to produce electricity. If Consumer i is given access to a plant of capacity k, then she can produce $x_i \leq k$ at the operating cost of $c_i x_i$. If $v_i'(k) > c_i$, then it would be wasteful not to fully utilize capacity, i.e., x_i should then be chosen to equal k, with a net benefit of $v_i(k) - c_i k$, and a corresponding net marginal benefit of $v_i'(k) - c_i$: expanding capacity allows Consumer i to increase her net benefit by $v_i'(k) - c_i$. Hence, $v_i'(k) - c_i$ is Consumer i's marginal valuation of capacity whenever $v_i'(k) > c_i$. But if $v_i'(k) \leq c_i$, then Consumer i does not benefit from an expansion of capacity, and her or his marginal valuation of capacity is zero.

Summarizing, Consumer i's *marginal valuation of capacity* is defined by

$$\hat{v}_i'(k) = \max\{v_i'(k) - c_i, 0\}, i = B, R, \tag{5.9}$$

which generalizes (5.2). Efficient pricing then allocates capacity costs according to (5.4) and (5.5), where k^* is implicitly defined by the Samuelson condition (5.3) for the marginal valuation functions (5.9).

Efficient prices for good X are then given by

$$p_i = \varphi_i + c_i = \hat{v}_i'(k^*) + c_i, i = B, R. \tag{5.10}$$

Case 1: $x_B^* > x_R^*$.

Blue (peak) fully utilizes capacity, where Red underutilizes it and, therefore, the marginal valuation of capacity by Red is zero. Capacity k^* equals x_B^* in this case, and hence $\hat{v}_R'(k^*) = 0$. Therefore, (5.6) and (5.7) apply, with personalized prices for good X given by (5.10), and (5.8) becomes:

$$p_B = \varphi + c_B = v_B'(x_B^*) = \hat{v}_B'(x_B^*) + c_B,$$

and

$$p_R = c_R = v_R'(x_R^*) = 0 + c_R.$$

Intuitively, if we want to increase peak supply x_B in one unit, then we must incur a marginal peak-time operating cost c_B plus the marginal capacity cost φ, whereas the incremental cost of increasing x_R in one unit is only c_R, its marginal operating cost. Efficiency requires equating the marginal valuations to the so-defined marginal costs. As in Section 5.2.2, this case parallels Figure 4.10 in Chapter 4 above.

Case 2: $x_B^* = x_R^*$.

Now capacity $k^* = x_B^* = x_R^*$, and (5.10) can be written as

$$p_i = \varphi_i + c_i = \hat{v}_i'(k^*) + c_i = v_i'(x_i^*), i = B, R.$$

As in Section 5.2.2, this case is similar to that of Figure 4.9 in Chapter 4 above.

Summarizing:

1. *The price of each period (or consumer) must cover at least the period's marginal operating cost.*
2. *The sum of the two prices must exactly cover all marginal costs (operating and capacity).*
3. *If capacity is not fully utilized during the off-peak period, then the marginal capacity cost is fully covered by the peak-period user.*
4. *If capacity is fully utilized in the off-peak period (i.e., the consumption level in either period equals the capacity level), then marginal capacity costs are distributed between the two periods according to rule:*

   Capacity price for i = i's Marginal valuation of capacity,

   in accordance with the principles for efficient pricing of a continuous public good when capacity is interpreted as a public good.

5.3   Capacity as a Yes–No variable and natural monopoly

5.3.1   Increasing returns in the production of a private good

We now consider a good X produced under strongly increasing returns to scale. We may think of good X as a communication or transportation service, which may be supplied by a public agency, a private, regulated firm, or a private firm in a (partially) deregulated environment: these instances are traditionally labeled *natural monopoly*. We analyse the conflict between efficiency and breaking even under increasing returns.

We postulate the marginal operating costs are the same for Blue and Red, i.e., $c_B = c_R = c$. Again as in Chapter 2 above, the cost depends only on the sum x of the quantities x_B and x_R, i.e., the cost function is written $C(x)$, where $x = x_B + x_R$. As usual, producing nothing costs nothing, i.e., $C(0) = 0$. But now we assume that producing any positive quantity $x > 0$ requires a fixed (overhead) cost F plus a variable cost, cx, that is proportional to the quantity, i.e.,

$$C(x) = \begin{cases} 0 \text{ if } x = 0, \\ F + cx \text{ if } x > 0, \end{cases}$$

see Figure 5.1. We can think of F as being the cost of building a Yes–No plant or infrastructure, of a given fixed size and characteristics. If the plant is not built, then good X cannot be produced. But if built, any amount of good X can be produced at a unit variable cost c, where c is a constant marginal (and average variable) cost. Because the average cost, $c + F/x$, is decreasing in x, the technology presents increasing returns to scale.

The social surplus function is now:

$$S(x_B, x_R): = \begin{cases} 0, \text{ if } x_B = x_R = 0, \\ v_B(x_B) + v_R(x_R) - F - cx_B - cx_R, \text{ if } x_B + x_R > 0. \end{cases} \tag{5.11}$$

It could happen that F is very high relative to valuations so that social surplus $v_B(x_B) + v_R(x_R) - F - cx_B - cx_R$ is always negative for nonzero x_B and x_R. It would then be efficient not to supply the good, reaching zero surplus. We rule this occurrence out by postulating that social surplus is actually positive for some nonzero (x_B, x_R), and, *a fortiori*, for the surplus-maximizing quantities: we call this the *viability condition*.

As in Chapters 1 and 2 above, efficiency requires the maximization of surplus (5.11). Assuming that surplus is maximized at a point where the consumption of good X by Blue and Red is positive, efficiency then implies (in addition to production efficiency) the marginal equalities (2.2) and (2.3) of Chapter 2 above between marginal valuations and marginal cost, which now become

$$v'_B(x_B) = c, \tag{5.12}$$

$$v'_R(x_R) = c. \tag{5.13}$$

Write x^*_B (resp. x^*_B) for the solution to (5.12) (resp. (5.13)), and $x^* := x^*_B + x^*_R$.

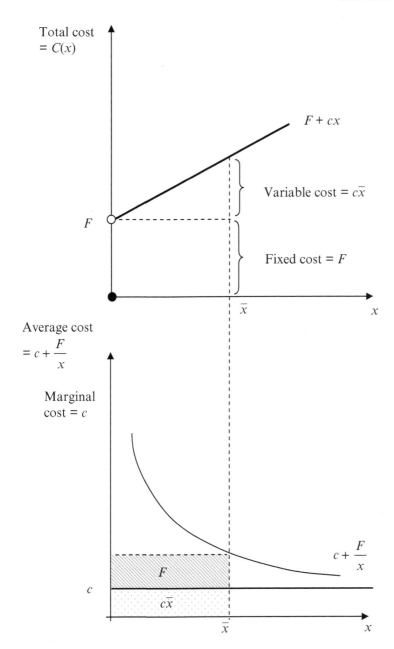

Figure 5.1 *Fixed cost and constant marginal cost*

5.3.2   Uniform and linear prices: the conflict between efficiency and breaking even

Assume now, as is customary, that consumers can buy any quantity they want at a market price p per unit. This is in fact a triple assumption. First, pricing is *linear*, meaning that the price per unit faced by an individual is the same no matter how many units she buys (in particular, no quantity discounts or surcharges, or two-part tariffs).[3] Second, pricing is *uniform*, meaning that every individual faces the same pricing schedule (the opposite of *personalized* pricing).[4] Third, *there is no rationing*: each consumer obtains the quantity that she demands at p.

Given the price p, we have, as in Section 2.4.1 of Chapter 2 above, that the quantities x_B and x_R that Blue and Red buy satisfy

$$v'_B(x_B) = p,$$

$$v'_R(x_R) = p.$$

Hence, from (5.12) and (5.13) efficiency (equivalent to surplus maximization) requires

$$p = c, \tag{5.14}$$

i.e., the price faced by consumers must equal the marginal cost.

We can adapt the graphs of Sections 2.4.4 and 2.4.5 of Chapter 2 above recalling that now we have a fixed cost, and therefore

Profits = Revenue – Variable cost – Fixed cost
= Producer surplus – Fixed cost.

Hence

Social surplus = Aggregate consumer surplus + Profits
= Aggregate consumer surplus + Producer surplus – F.

Figure 5.2 illustrates. Because efficiency requires pricing at marginal cost (i.e., $p = c$, see (5.14)), and because marginal cost c is lower than average cost ($c + F/x$), a remarkable conclusion emerges:

---

[3] One sometimes refers to this assumption as the absence of *second degree price discrimination.*

[4] One sometimes refers to this assumption as the absence of *third degree price discrimination. First degree discrimination* means that both second and third degree are present.

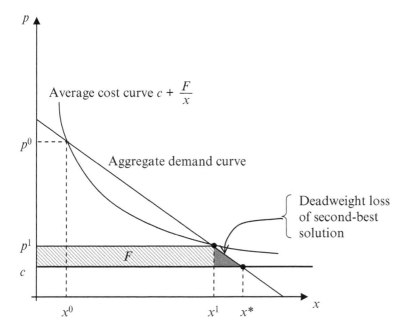

Figure 5.2 *Efficiency and second best under linear, uniform prices*

If prices are restricted to be linear, then efficiency implies losses.

Indeed, price equals marginal cost at x^* in Figure 5.2, where producer surplus is zero and profits equal minus F, i.e., the firm covers only its variable cost, and it suffers losses by the amount of the fixed cost F. Losses are not necessarily an indication of mismanagement but, on the contrary, they just follow from economic efficiency!

In order to achieve efficiency, the firm must be subsidized by the amount F. This solution, sometimes adopted when the public sector owns the utility, is not without problems. First, the taxpayer has to ultimately pay the subsidy. Thus, the efficient operation of the firm may require a transfer from taxpayers to users, which may be inequitable. Second, in real life the magnitude of the fixed cost F may be unknown to the public authority, and, thus, it may be in practice difficult to distinguish the losses mandated by economic efficiency from those caused by mismanagement. The firm could, in particular, engage in a variety of wasteful activities, knowing that all losses will be eventually covered by subsidies: this phenomenon has been dubbed the "soft budget constraint" by Janos Kornai.[5]

If these considerations become dominant, then the firm may be required to break even. Efficiency is, then, impossible, and one can only hope for a *second-best* solution, i.e., the highest surplus consistent with nonnegative profits, as discussed in Section 4.5.3 and Appendix 4A above for the case of public goods. Graphically (see Figure 5.2) this amounts to finding the quantity that generates the highest surplus among those between x^0 and x^1. The solution is, obviously, x^1. Profits are zero (i.e., producer surplus equals the fixed cost F), and the outcome is inefficient: the shaded triangle depicts the deadweight loss of the second-best solution.

So far we have assumed that prices are uniform (everybody faces the same pricing schedule) and linear (what you pay is price times quantity). Under these conditions, economic efficiency implies that the firm cannot break even. The next section shows how the conflict can be addressed by means of nonlinear pricing.[6]

5.3.3   Two-part tariffs

We consider the simplest form of nonlinear pricing, namely a two-part tariff. In order to develop the intuition for the analysis of two-part tariffs,

---

[5] J. Kornai (1980), *Economics of Shortage*, Amsterdam: North-Holland.
[6] Appendix 5B below studies a way of mitigating this conflict with linear, personalized prices.

consider the extreme case where $c = 0$, so that the only cost is the fixed cost F. This extreme case is very similar to the Yes–No public good discussed in Section 4.5.3 of Chapter 4 above. Indeed, providing the facility requires a cost of F, but, once provided, the good can be made available to consumers in any amounts at zero additional cost. The fixed cost F is the cost of *an input which, if present, permits the production and consumption of any quantities of the good with no additional cost.* If, on the contrary, the input is absent, then the good cannot be produced. Accordingly, the input can be called the "ability to produce good X" and has the character of an indivisible public good, with $\overline{C} = F$ in the notation of Section 4.5.3 of Chapter 4 above.

If the marginal cost of producing good X were zero, then Blue would consume the quantity x_B^* for which the marginal valuation is zero, i.e., x_B^* satisfies "$v_B'(x_B^*) = 0$," and she would be willing to pay up to $A_B := v_B(x_B^*)$ for it. Accordingly, $v_B(x_B^*)$ is Blue's valuation of the input, parallel to the valuation $\overline{v}_B$ of the public good in Section 4.5.3.

The situation is a little more complex when $c > 0$. Then the fixed cost F is the cost of an input interpreted as the "ability to produce good X at an operating cost of c per unit." Consumer i's payment for x_i units of the good consists now of two parts:

1. A fixed part, denoted A_i and called an *access fee* that she (or he) must pay if she wants to consume the good at all, and
2. A variable part which is proportional to x_i, i.e., $p_i x_i$, where p_i is *is* (constant) *marginal price* or *marginal fee*.

In other words, if Consumer i does not want to buy the good, then she pays nothing. But if she wants to buy a positive quantity x_i, then she must pay $A_i + p_i x_i$. If the numbers A_i and p_i are the same for everybody, then we say that the pricing scheme is uniform.

We ask: *Is it possible to achieve economic efficiency while the firm breaks even?* Our conclusions, analogous to those of the Yes–No public good analysis in Section 4.5.3 above, will be:

1. *Economic efficiency requires, in any event, that $p_i = c$, i.e., everybody's marginal price must equal the marginal cost.* (In particular, the marginal price must be uniform.)[7]
2. *It is always possible to achieve economic efficiency while the firm breaks even by means of a personalized access fee, together with a uniform marginal price equal to the marginal cost.*

---

[7] We disregard in this section the possibility of vertical segments (as the one in Figure 5B.1 in Appendix 5B below) in a consumer's demand curve.

3. *If utility functions are very different, then the access fees must be personalized in order to achieve economic efficiency while the firm breaks even.*
4. *If utility functions are not too different, then a uniform access fee, together with a uniform marginal price equal to the marginal cost, achieves economic efficiency while the firm breaks even.*

Consider the case of two consumers. Efficiency requires that the marginal price be equal to the marginal cost c. Then, the firm will break even only when the access fees add up to the fixed cost F, i.e., A_B and A_R (for Ms. Blue and Mr. Red, respectively) and satisfy the *break-even condition*:

$$A_B + A_R = F. \qquad (5.15)$$

But, in order to achieve efficiency, the access fees cannot be so high as to discourage anybody from accessing. Recall from Section 5.3.1 above that x_B^* and x_R^* are respectively defined by the equations $v_B'(*x_B) = c$ and $v_R'(*x_R) = c$. Define CS_B^* and CS_R^* by

$$CS_B^* := v_B(x_B^*) - cx_B^*, \qquad (5.16)$$

$$CS_R^* =: v_R(x_R^*) - cx_R^*, \qquad (5.17)$$

i.e., CS_B^* (resp. CS_R^*) is the *consumer surplus obtained by Blue (resp. Red) at a linear price equal to c.*

We can interpret CS_B^* as *Blue's valuation of the ability to buy at price c* by the following reasoning. Given the two-part schedule defined by A_B and $p_B = c$, Blue can either participate or not. The net benefit of not participating is zero. If she does participate, then she will buy x_B^*. Thus, her net benefit if she does participate is $CS_B^* - A_B$. Accordingly, she participates only if

$$CS_B^* \geq A_B,$$

a condition called, as in Section 4.5.3 above, Blue's *participation constraint* (see (4.18)). A similar condition applies to Red.

Putting together the break-even condition (5.15) and the participation constraints we have

$$A_B + A_R = F,$$

$$CS_B^* \geq A_B, \tag{5.18}$$

$$CS_R^* \geq A_R. \tag{5.19}$$

Comparing with the Yes–No excludable public good that was discussed in Section 4.5.3 above, we see that valuations of the public good by the consumers there (denoted $\bar{v}_i$, $i = B, R$, in Section 4.5.3), are now the CS_B^* and CS_R^* of (5.16) and (5.17). Thus, (5.15), (5.18) and (5.19) of this section parallel (4.19) and (4.18) of Section 4.5.3. And the viability condition of this section parallels inequality (4.17) of Section 4.5.3.

The question: "Is it possible to achieve efficiency while the firm breaks even?" can now be rephrased as: "*Is it possible to find access fees that satisfy both the break-even and the participation conditions for the surplus-maximizing amounts?*"

The analysis proceeds exactly as in Section 4.5.3. If we allow for personalized access fees, i.e., for $A_B \neq A_R$, then the answer is Yes. The argument goes as follows: the viability assumption implies that maximal surplus is positive, i.e.,

$$CS_B^* + CS_R^* > F. \tag{5.20}$$

Thus, it is certainly possible to divide the fixed cost F into two fees, A_B and A_R, satisfying $A_B \leq CS_B^*$ and $A_R \leq CS_R^*$. Figure 5.3 illustrates: it parallels Figure 4.11 of Chapter 4 above. Consider the point with coordinates CS_B^* and CS_R^*. Pairs of access fees (A_B, A_R) southwest of this point satisfy the participation constraints (shaded area). The coordinates of points on the FF line add up to the fixed cost F: therefore, pairs of access fees (A_B, A_R) on the FF line satisfy the break-even condition. Because of (5.20), the point with coordinates CS_B^* and CS_R^* lies northeast of the line FF, and, thus, the line intersects the shaded rectangle. Any pair of access fees (A_B, A_R) on the intersection (i.e., on the solid segment) does the job. As a particular example, let:

$$A_B = \frac{CS_B^*}{CS_B^* + CS_R^*} F, \text{ and } A_R = \frac{CS_R^*}{CS_B^* + CS_R^*} F.$$

If people have different valuation functions, then the solid segment may not include the point with both coordinates equal to $F/2$. In this case, illustrated in Figure 5.3(a), the attainment of efficiency while covering costs necessitates personalized access fees. But if CS_B^* and CS_R^* are not too different, then they both may be greater than $F/2$, and the uniform access fee $A = A_B = A_R = F/2$ does the trick, see Figure 5.3(b).

The second-best question of maximizing surplus subject to the conditions that the firm breaks even and access fees are uniform has the same

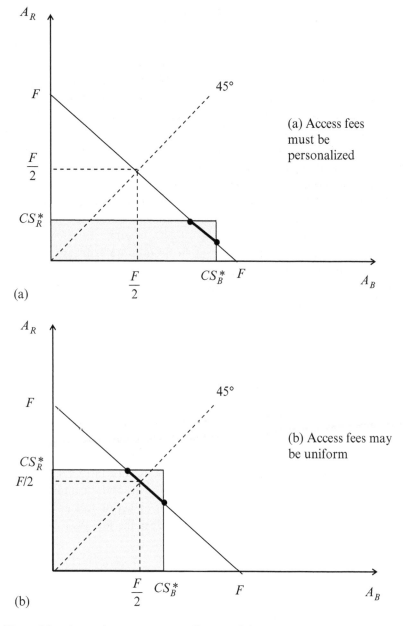

Figure 5.3   *Access fees guaranteeing efficiency while covering costs*

answer as in Section 4.5.3 above. If, for instance, $CS_R^* < F/2$ and $CS_B^* \geq F$, then the second-best solution sets $A = F$, with only Blue accessing. But if the data are as in Figure 5.3(a), then the second-best solution entails not supplying the good.

Appendix 5A   Access fees in the continuum economy

The parallelism between excludable, Yes–No public goods and fixed costs carries over to the continuum economy. A bridge of a given size and design, not subject to congestion or wear-and-tear, can be visualized as an excludable public good, which can be supplied at a cost of $\overline{C}$ and possibly financed by access tolls. But it can also be visualized as the provision of a private good, namely "bridge crossings," with large fixed costs of $F = \overline{C}$ and zero marginal costs.

Let the interval $(0, N_0]$ denote the set of potential bridge users: a user may cross the bridge once (Yes) or not at all (No): as before, $\bar{v}(n)$ denotes Person n's valuation of crossing the bridge. The analysis is identical to that in Appendix 4A above. Efficiency can be achieved under personalized tolls. But if tolls have to be uniform, positive tolls may discourage people with small but positive $\bar{v}(n)$ resulting in inefficiency. And the second-best problem of maximizing social surplus subject to covering costs with a uniform toll may imply either an inefficiently low number of users, or even, depending on the parameters, not building the bridge at all.

Appendix 5B   Personalized linear prices and the Ramsey–Boiteux equation

Suppose now that it is possible to charge different people personalized prices, but prices still have to be linear. Because now the option of charging different prices is available, one should expect that the conflict between efficiency and breaking even may be somewhat attenuated. To what extent and in what way? Our conclusions will be:

1. In the exceptional, extreme case where a consumer (or segment of the market) has perfectly inelastic demand, efficiency may be achieved while covering costs by marking up the price for the inelastic consumer.
2. Except for this extreme case, efficiency is still incompatible with breaking even.
3. Nevertheless, charging different prices allows for an increase in social surplus, i.e., an allocation can be attained which yields a social surplus higher than what could be achieved with linear, uniform prices under the break-even constraint.
4. The second-best solution (i.e., the one that maximizes surplus subject to the break-even constraint) imposes a personalized markup over marginal cost, with a *higher markup for the consumer with relatively more inelastic demand.*

To argue (1), consider the exceptional case depicted in Figure 5B.1. The surplus-maximizing quantity is $x^* := x_B^* + x_R^*$. What is peculiar in this example is Ms. Blue's utility: her demand curve is, within some price limits, perfectly inelastic.[8] Efficiency is achieved when Mr. Red consumes x_R^* units of electricity and Ms. Blue consumes x_B^* units. But Ms. Blue will still buy x_B^* units if her personalized price is higher than the marginal cost. One can exploit this fact (and, in a sense, Ms. Blue) to achieve efficiency while covering costs. To this end, charge Mr. Red the price $p_R = c$, and Ms. Blue the price $p_B = c + F/x_B^*$. If the vertical segment of Ms. Blue is high enough, she will still demand the amount x_B^*, so that efficiency is achieved, while the revenues of the firm exactly cover costs.[9]

But, except for this exceptional case, a price higher than marginal cost will induce consumers to buy quantities lower than what they would buy at marginal cost, making efficiency incompatible with covering costs. The idea of charging a higher price for the person (or market segment) with

---

[8] Ms. Blue's utility is a peculiar function because her marginal valuation is not well defined at x_B^*. In other words, her valuation function $v_B(x_B)$ has a kink at x_B^*, and is not differentiable there.

[9] The fairness of this solution is, of course, a completely different issue.

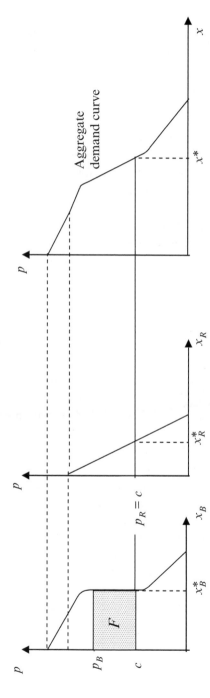

Figure 5B.1 *The extreme case of a perfectly inelastic demand curve: efficiency can be achieved by linear, personalized prices*

a relatively rigid demand is, however, fruitful even in this case, because it allows for a second-best level of surplus higher than the one achieved under uniform (linear) prices depicted in Figure 5.2. The second-best solution with personalized prices is given by the *Ramsey–Boiteux* equation.[10]

We can derive it by using the method of Lagrange multipliers. Write $\tilde{x}_B(p_B)$ and $\tilde{x}_R(p_R)$ respectively, for Blue's and Red's demand function (found by solving the equations $p_B = v_B'(x_B)$ and $p_R = v_R'(x_R)$ respectively). The problem is to choose p_B and p_R in order to:

$$\text{maximize } v_B(\tilde{x}_B(p_B)) + v_R(\tilde{x}_R(p_R)) - F - c\tilde{x}_B(p_B) - c\tilde{x}_R(p_R)$$

$$\text{subject to } p_B\tilde{x}_B(p_B) + p_R\tilde{x}_R(p_R) = F + c\tilde{x}_B(p_B) + c\tilde{x}_R(p_R).$$

A first order condition of this problem is that, for some endogenous Lagrange multiplier $\lambda \geq 0$:

$$[v_i' - c]\tilde{x}_i' + \lambda[\tilde{x}_i + p_i\tilde{x}_i' - c\tilde{x}_i'] = 0, \quad i = B, R,$$

or recalling that, in the absence of rationing, $v_i' = p_i$,

$$[1 + \lambda][p_i - c]\tilde{x}_i' = -\lambda\tilde{x}_i, \quad i = B, R.$$

If $\tilde{x}_i' = 0$ (demand perfectly inelastic), then $\lambda = 0$ (the break-even constraint is not binding). Otherwise, we obtain:

$$\frac{p_i - c}{p_i} = \frac{\lambda}{1 + \lambda}\left[-\frac{\tilde{x}_i}{\tilde{x}_i'p_i}\right], \quad i = B, R.$$

Write $\varepsilon_i := -\tilde{x}_i'p_i/\tilde{x}_i$, the absolute value of the price elasticity of the (direct) demand function. Then the expression becomes the Ramsey–Boiteux equation:

$$\frac{p_i - c}{p_i} = \frac{\dfrac{\lambda}{1 + \lambda}}{\varepsilon_i}, \quad i = B, R.$$

In particular, as long as $\lambda > 0$ (i.e., the break-even constraint is binding) and $0 < \varepsilon_i < \infty$ (demand is neither perfectly inelastic nor perfectly elastic):

1. $p_i - c > 0$, i.e., everybody is charged a price higher than marginal cost.
2. $p_h < p_i$ if and only if $\varepsilon_h > \varepsilon_i$, i.e., the consumer or market with the more elastic demand pays less.

Figure 5B.1 corresponds to the limit as $\varepsilon_B \to 0$, whereas $\varepsilon_R > 0$. Then $\lambda \to 0$ and $p_R \to c$.

---

[10] Named after Frank P. Ramsey (1903–1930) and Marcel Boiteux (born 1922).

6 Uncertainty and asymmetrical information

● ●

6.1 Decisions under uncertainty

Many real-life decisions, both by individuals and by the public sector, are made under conditions of uncertainty: the outcome of a given decision is influenced by a random event. Consider a consumer faced with choosing between two free gifts: one is an amount $\overline{m}$ of numeraire, the other one is a lottery ticket, which with probability $[1 - \pi]$ gives a prize of m^H units of numeraire, and with probability π gives nothing. To fix ideas, think of the value of a unit of numeraire to be one dollar, and m^H to be one million, let $\pi = 0.5$; i.e., if you own the ticket, a fair coin is tossed you receive one million dollars if it lands heads, and nothing if it lands tails, and let $\overline{m} = 400,000$. Denoting by ω, as usual, the initial endowment of numeraire, there are three possible outcomes, all in units of numeraire: $\omega + m^H$ (obtained if you choose the ticket and the coin lands on heads), ω (obtained if you choose the ticket and the coin lands on tails), and $\omega + \overline{m}$ (if you choose the cash gift). Figure 6.1, called a *decision tree*, illustrates: at the square, the consumer has to decide Ticket or Cash gift, whereas at the circle fate, or nature, chooses Tails or Heads. The various outcomes, or amounts of numeraire, are then determined by the consumer' s decision together with the random event resulting from the coin toss.

Will you choose Ticket or Cash gift? The choice will obviously depend on the numbers m^H and $\overline{m}$, but also on π, and possibly on ω. In addition, different people, even facing the same m^H, $\overline{m}$, π and ω, may choose differently. Perhaps Blue chooses the cash gift, whereas Red chooses the ticket: either choice may be perfectly rational given the person's preferences, and, in particular, her or his degree of risk aversion. In particular, we may say that these choices are consistent with Blue being *more risk averse* than Red.

In the previous example, one of two random events or states of the world occurs, namely Tails or Heads. Under uncertainty, decisions have to be made *before* the state of the world is known: using the Latin term for "before," they are called decisions *ex ante*. Similarly, the utility function that controls these decisions is called the *ex ante* utility function: it is

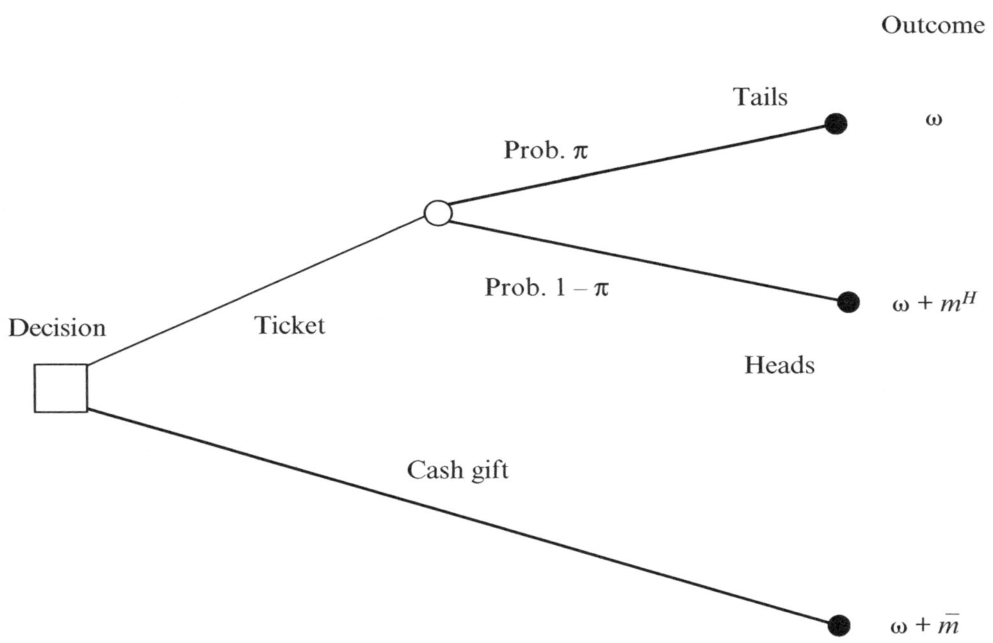

Figure 6.1 *Decision tree for Ticket vs. Cash gift*

important to understand that the arguments in the *ex ante* utility function are not outcomes (i.e., amounts of numeraire), but decisions (alternatives or actions: in the example, Ticket or Cash gift).

6.2 Prices vs. quantities in externality policy

Section 3.2.9 above argued the equivalence, under certainty, of Pigouvian taxes (a *price* policy) and cap-and-trade mechanisms (a *quantity* policy) as instruments to induce efficiency in the presence of negative externalities. But the equivalence breaks down when there is uncertainty or imperfect information on the costs or benefits of the externality causing activity.[1]

We go back to the Blue and Red example of Section 3.2.1 above (no abatement), with utility functions

$$U_B(x_B, m_B) = \sqrt{v_B(x_B)} + m_B,$$

$$U_R(x_R, Z, m_R) = \sqrt{v_R(x_R)} + m_R - \gamma(Z), \text{ where } Z = x_B.$$

The external cost or damage function $\gamma(Z)$ is of the form

$$\gamma(Z) = \eta Z + 0.5\,\zeta Z^2,$$

with marginal external cost $\gamma'(Z) = \eta + \zeta Z$. This generalizes the formulation of external cost of Chapter 3 above, which corresponds to $\eta = g$ and $\zeta = 0$. Here we postulate that $\eta = 0$ and $\zeta > 0$.

We assume for simplicity that Blue's marginal (internal) benefit is

$$v'_B(x_B) = a_B - x_B,$$

(with slope $-b_B = -1$) and that the resource cost of producing good X is zero, i.e., $c = 0$.

External damages are often researched by science, and the relevant information may be available to the policy maker, while the internal benefits of the externality-causing agent may be private information, on which the policy maker may not have precise knowledge. To model this situation, we postulate that the policy maker knows the external cost function $\gamma(Z)$

---

[1] The analysis, pioneered by Martin Weitzman (1974), "Prices vs. quantities," *Review of Economic Studies*, 41(4), 477–491, can be extended to the costs and benefits of mitigation, abatement or adaptation.

with certainty, but is uncertain on Blue's marginal benefit, more specifically on the parameter a_B: it may turn out to be

- a high a_B^H with probability 0.5, or
- a low a_B^L, also with probability 0.5.

The policy maker chooses between a cap-and-trade policy with $\bar{x}$ permits issued, and a linear tax policy at rate $\bar{t}$. But the policy must be chosen *ex ante*, without knowing whether the realized (Latin, *ex post*) value of a_B is a_B^H or a_B^L. We assume that the *ex post* value of a_B is later found out by Blue, who decides on x_B (which equals Z) in view of the policy. Blue's decision then determines the realized, or *ex post*, level of social surplus. Figure 6.2 displays the decision tree of the policy maker.

If the policy maker chooses a cap-and-trade (quantity) policy $\bar{x}$, then Blue sets $x_B = Z = \bar{x}$, and *ex post* surplus is, neglecting the invariant term $v_R(x_R^*)$

- $a_B^H \bar{x} - 0.5\bar{x}^2 - 0.5\zeta\bar{x}^2$, if the *ex post* value of a_B is a_B^H, and
- $a_B^L \bar{x} - 0.5\bar{x}^2 - 0.5\zeta\bar{x}^2$, if the *ex post* value of a_B is a_B^L.

We assume that the policy maker maximizes expected, or average, surplus, computed as

$$0.5\,[a_B^H \bar{x} - 0.5\bar{x}^2 - 0.5\zeta\bar{x}^2] + 0.5\,[a_B^L \bar{x} - 0.5\bar{x}^2 - 0.5\zeta\bar{x}^2]$$
$$= 0.5\,[a_B^H + a_B^L]\bar{x} - 0.5\bar{x}^2 - 0.5\zeta\bar{x}^2, \tag{6.1}$$

with first order condition $0.5[a_B^H + a_B^L] - \bar{x} - \zeta\bar{x} = 0$, i.e., when choosing cap and trade, the policy maker issues the amount of permits:

$$\bar{x} = \frac{0.5[a_B^H + a_B^L]}{1 + \zeta}. \tag{6.2}$$

But if the policy maker adopts a tax (price) policy with marginal tax rate t, then Blue *ex post* chooses the following amounts of good X:

$$x_B^H = a_B^H - t \text{ if the } ex\ post \text{ value of } a_B \text{ is } a_B^H,$$

and

$$x_B^L = a_B^L - t \text{ if the } ex\ post \text{ value of } a_B \text{ is } a_B^H.$$

Hence, the expected surplus under a tax t is

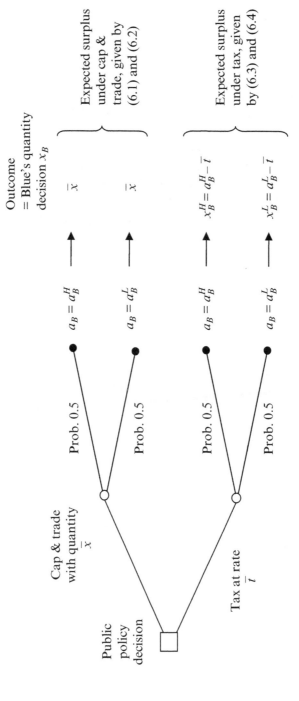

Figure 6.2 *Decision tree for externality policies under uncertainty*

$$0.5\,[a_B^H x_B^H - 0.5[x_B^H]^2 - 0.5\zeta\,[x_B^H]^2] + 0.5\,[a_B^L x_B^L - 0.5[x_B^L]^2 - 0.5\zeta[x_B^L]^2]$$
$$= 0.5\,[a_B^H[a_B^H - t] - 0.5[1 + \zeta][a_B^H - t]^2]$$
$$+ 0.5\,[a_B^L[a_B^L - t] - 0.5[1 + \zeta][a_B^L - t]^2].$$

Differentiating this expression with respect to t, we find the first-order condition of the maximization of expected surplus under the tax policy:

$$0.5\,[\,-a_B^H + [1 + \zeta][a_B^H - t]] + 0.5\,[\,-a_B^L + [1 + \zeta][a_B^L - t]] = 0,$$

i.e.,

$$\bar{t} = \frac{0.5[a_B^H + a_B^L]\zeta}{1 + \zeta}. \tag{6.3}$$

We can see from (6.1)–(6.3) that the policy maker acts as if the marginal benefit curve were the average $0.5[a_B^H + a_B^L] - x_B$: see the dashed, downward sloping line between the high and low marginal benefit curves in Figure 6.3.

What yields a higher expected surplus, a cap-and-trade system with quantity $\bar{x}$ or a Pigouvian tax at rate $\bar{t}$?

Fact (Weitzman, 1974). A cap-and-trade system is preferable to a tax if and only if $1 < \zeta$ (i.e., the marginal internal benefit is flatter *than the marginal external cost).*

Figure 6.3 illustrates the argument. Figure 6.3(a) depicts the case where the marginal internal benefit is *flatter* than the marginal external cost, i.e., $1 < \zeta$. First, let the *ex post* value of a_B be a_B^H. The *ex post* marginal benefit curve is then the higher one, crossing the marginal cost curve at point B. On the one hand, cap-and-trade yields $x_B = Z = \bar{x}$, which is inefficiently *low*, generating an *ex post* deadweight loss equal to the area of triangle EAB. On the other hand, a tax rate $\bar{t}$ induces Blue to choose x_B^H, which is inefficiently *high*, with an *ex post* deadweight loss equal to the area of triangle BCD, larger than that of triangle EAB. The same result obtains when the *ex post* value of a_B turns out to be a_B^L, and Blue chooses x_B^L when facing the tax policy $\bar{t}$. Hence, if $1 < \zeta$, then a cap-and-trade policy yields a higher expected surplus than a tax policy.

Figure 6.3(b) depicts the opposite case, where the marginal internal benefit is *steeper* than the marginal external cost, i.e., $1 > \zeta$. When the *ex post* value of a_B is a_B^H, cap and trade generates an *ex post* deadweight loss equal to the area of triangle $E'A'B'$, which is now larger than that of $B'C'D'$, the *ex post* deadweight loss of the tax policy $\bar{t}$. Hence, when $1 > \zeta$, a tax is preferable to cap and trade.

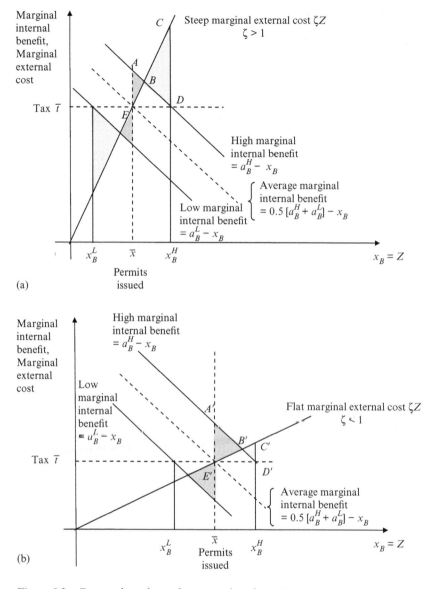

Figure 6.3   *Expected surplus under cap-and-trade vs. Pigouvian taxes*

6.3 Asymmetrical information and adverse selection

Recall the conditions of First Fundamental Theorem of Welfare Economics (Section 2.3 above). Chapters 3 and 4 have discussed externalities and public goods. We now focus on the symmetry of information, which requires that all parties engaged in market transactions be equally informed: buyers and sellers of a good must have the same information about its characteristics. If one party has better information than the other one, then the First Fundamental Theorem of Welfare Economics does not apply, and the allocation obtained at the market equilibrium will typically be inefficient.

This fact is particularly relevant for insurance markets. But the basic idea, due to George Akerlof, can be presented as follows.[2] Consider a hypothetical island with 320 inhabitants: 100 of them are old, and 220 young. Each of 50 old people owns two cars of good quality, called "peaches," and each of the other 50 old people owns two cars of bad quality, called "lemons." No young person initially owns a car. We assume that the only goods in the island are cars and the numeraire, and that the utility function of Person i is as follows (people are numbered from $i = 1$ to $i = 320$):

$1650 + m_i$, if i is old and ends up with a peach and m_i units of numeraire,
$3150 + m_i$, if i is old and ends up with two peaches and m_i units of numeraire (i.e., the second peach is worth 1500 to her),
$1000 + m_i$, if i is old and ends up with a lemon and m_i units of numeraire,
$2650 + m_i$, if i is old and ends up with a lemon, a peach and m_i units of numeraire,
$2000 + m_i$, if i is old and ends up with two lemons and m_i units of numeraire,
$2100 + m_i$, if i is young and ends up with a peach and m_i units of numeraire,
$1100 + m_i$, if i is young and ends up with a lemon and m_i units of numeraire.

Assume that a second car has no value for a young person. Clearly, economic efficiency (or surplus maximization) requires all cars to end up in the hands of young people, who value cars more highly. But does the market reach an efficient allocation?

---

[2] G. Akerlof (1970), "The market for 'lemons': Quality uncertainty and the market mechanism," *Quarterly Journal of Economics*, 84(3), 488–500. Akerlof (born 1940) was awarded the 2001 Nobel Prize in Economic Sciences.

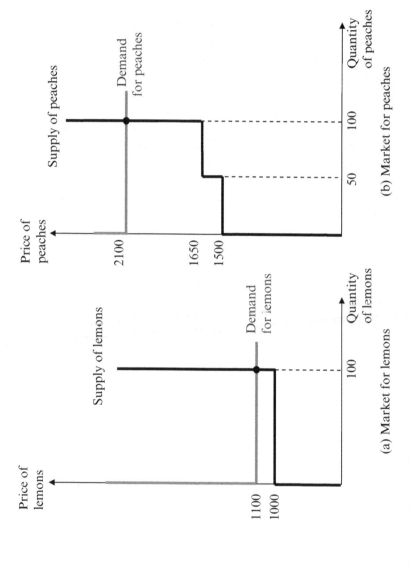

Figure 6.4 *Symmetrical, good information*

Case 1: Information is symmetrical and good
Then the conditions of the First Fundamental Theorem of Welfare Economics are satisfied, and thus the theorem guarantees the efficiency of the equilibrium allocation. If everybody can tell a peach from a lemon, then there are two separate markets, one for lemons and one for peaches, see Figure 6.4. The supply curves are defined by the reservation prices for lemons and for peaches of the sellers (old people). The demand curves require more attention, because the demand for lemons may depend on the price of peaches, and vice versa. But if, say, the peach market is in equilibrium, with 100 peaches demanded, then there is a potential demand of up to 120 lemons at the reservation price for a lemon by a young person (1100), yielding the demand curve of Figure 6.4(a). A similar argument applies to the market for peaches. We conclude that, in equilibrium, all 100 lemons are sold at the price of 1100 units of numeraire, and all 100 peaches are sold at 2100. (The equilibrium price is the reservation price of a young person, because there are more young people than cars.) All cars end up in the hands of young people, and hence the market equilibrium allocation is efficient.

We now consider the possibility of bad information, where a person cannot tell a lemon from a peach: there will be a single market, the market for cars. A person with bad information is then facing uncertainty: buying a car is in fact buying a lottery ticket that with some probability will yield a lemon and with the complementary probability a peach. Will she buy? Of course, this will depend on the probabilities and on the price p of a car: Figure 6.5 depicts her decision tree. We assume that her *ex ante* valuation equals her *expected valuation*, defined as:

[*Probability of the car being a lemon*] × [*Valuation of a lemon*]

+ [*Probability of the car being a peach*] × [*Valuation of a peach*].

Hence, if a young person has bad information and believes that the probability of a car being a lemon is μ, then she values a car at

$$\mu\,1100 + [1 - \mu]\,2100. \tag{6.4}$$

In a parallel manner, if a potential seller (i.e., an old person) has bad information about the cars that she owns, but she knows that one half of the old people own peaches, then her valuation of keeping only one car is

$$0.5 \times 1000 + 0.5 \times 1650 = 1325, \tag{6.5}$$

and her valuation of keeping a second car is

$$0.5 \times 1000 + 0.5 \times 1500 = 1250. \tag{6.6}$$

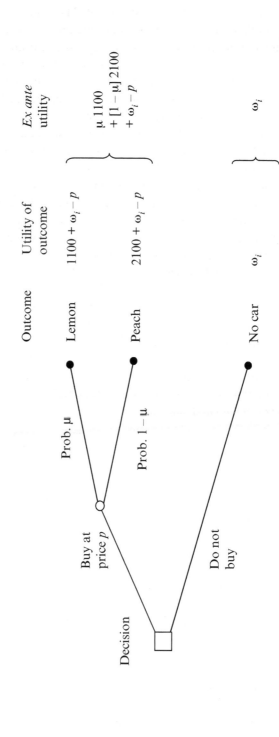

Figure 6.5 *Decision tree for a young person with bad information*

We add a condition to the concept of competitive market equilibrium. Not only must demand equal supply, but anybody with bad information must have, at equilibrium, a correct estimate of the *probabilities* of a car being a peach or a lemon. Hence, a seller with bad information must, as just stated, take the probability of a car being a lemon as 0.5. And if a buyer has bad information, then her estimate μ of the probability of getting a lemon *must equal the proportion of lemons among the cars actually offered in the market.*

Case 2: Information is symmetrical and bad

In this case, both buyers and sellers have bad information. Again, the conditions of the First Fundamental Theorem of Welfare Economics are satisfied, because the theorem does not require information to be perfect, just symmetrical, and the competitive market equilibrium is efficient.

An old person values her first car at 1325 and her second car at 1250 (by (6.5) and (6.6)), and all car sellers behave in the same manner in the market. Accordingly, any car offered for sale at or above 1325 has a $\mu = 0.5$ probability of being a lemon, and the valuation of a car by a young person is, according to (6.4), 1600. Figure 6.6 depicts the market equilibrium: all cars are sold to the young (at a price of 1600), resulting again in an efficient allocation.

Case 3: Asymmetrical information

Assume now that every old person knows whether she owns two peaches or two lemons, but young people cannot tell a peach from a lemon. The value of a car for a young person is given by (6.4), where μ must coincide with the fraction of lemons among the cars offered for sale. Note that, at least, $\mu = 0.5$, because if the price of a car is high enough to motivate the sale of any peach, then all lemons are also offered for sale. Hence, the value of a car to a young person cannot exceed 1600, and is less than 1600 if $\mu > 0.5$. But if the price is 1600 or less, at most 50 are peaches offered in the market, because each of the 50 owners of peaches is willing to sell both her peaches only if the price of a peach is greater than or equal to 1650. Hence, at most 50 cars offered at equilibrium would be peaches, implying that $\mu \geq 2/3$. But even if 50 peaches were offered, a young person would value a car at no more than $[2/3] \times 1100 + [1/3] \times 2100 < 1433$ (by (6.4)), and no old person would then sell her second peach, which she values at 1500. Hence, no peaches are offered at equilibrium. Buyers correctly conjecture that all cars are lemons, i.e., $\mu = 1$, and all lemons are sold at the equilibrium price of 1100, see Figure 6.7. No peach is transferred from old to young, and therefore the resulting allocation is inefficient.

The inefficiency of the market equilibrium under asymmetrical information is often referred to as the phenomenon of *adverse selection*: by a sort of Gresham' s law, lemons drive peaches out of the market.

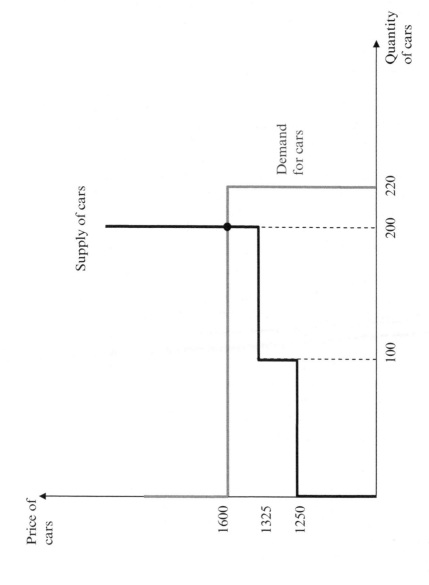

Figure 6.6 *Symmetrical, bad information*

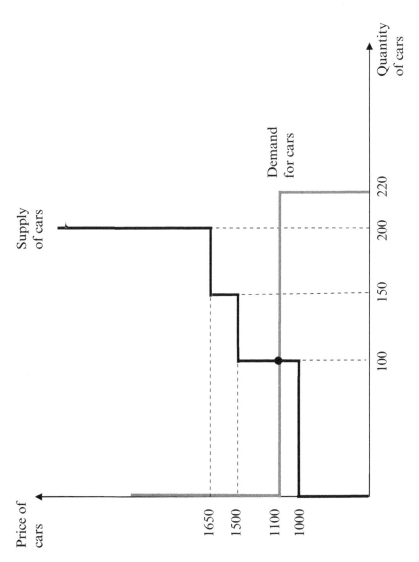

Figure 6.7 *Asymmetrical information*

A hypothetical policy that would restore efficiency would be "compulsory car sales," admittedly far-fetched in the car interpretation, but less so in the insurance problem to be discussed in Section 6.10 below: all cars are sold by law, achieving efficiency. But can everybody be better off under compulsory sales than at the market equilibrium, or, in the terms defined in Chapter 1 above, can a compulsory policy *Pareto dominate* the market equilibrium allocation?

There is no general answer to this question. The answer turns out to be affirmative in our numerical example, but it would be negative with other numbers. Suppose that the policy maker requires all old people to sell both their cars at a price of 1580 per car. The owner of two peaches loses 3150 (her valuation of her two cars) but gets a sales revenue of 2 × 1580 = 3160, with a net gain of 10, whereas at the market equilibrium her net gain was zero, because she sold nothing. The owner of two lemons is selling them at a substantially higher price than at equilibrium, so she is certainly better off. As for a young person, at the market equilibrium she is getting a lemon at her reservation price of 1100, and hence her net gain is zero, whereas under the compulsory policy she pays 1580 for a 50–50 chance of a lemon or a peach, which she values at 1600. So she wins too. Compulsion is here a win–win policy!

6.4 Risk aversion

Postulate for the remainder of this chapter a single consumption good, namely the numeraire, which we call "consumption." The *ex ante* preferences of real-life consumers often display *risk aversion*: a consumer often prefers a certain consumption of 75 to a 50–50 chance of consuming 50 or 100, where

$$75 = 0.5 \times 50 + 0.5 \times 100$$

$$= [Probability\ of\ consuming\ 50] \times 50$$

$$+ [Probability\ of\ consuming\ 100] \times 100.$$

More generally, we say that a consumer *displays risk aversion* (or is *risk averse*) if, when facing the choice between: (i) an uncertain (i.e., random) prospect of consuming the amount m^L with probability π, and the amount m^H with probability $[1 - \pi]$, and (ii) a certain (i.e., nonrandom) consumption of $\pi m^L + [1 - \pi] m^H$, she prefers (ii) to (i).

We call $\pi m^L + [1 - \pi] m^H$ the *expected consumption* of the uncertain prospect.

For the example of Section 6.1 above and Figure 6.1, risk aversion means that the consumer prefers the cash gift of $\overline{m} = \pi m^H$ to the lottery ticket. Note that when $\pi = 0.5$ and $m^H = 1,000,000$, then $\pi m^H = 500,000$. If Blue prefers the cash gift of $\overline{m} = 400,000$ to the ticket, then she displays risk aversion. But the fact that Red prefers the ticket to the cash gift of $\overline{m} = 400,000$ does not give us enough information: we should have him choose between the ticket and a cash gift of 500,000. If he preferred the 500,000, then he would display risk aversion, but if he were indifferent between the ticket and 500,000, then we would say that he displays *risk neutrality*.

As a second example, consider another hypothetical island in a far away ocean, divided into a western side and an eastern side by a mountain range. Ms. Blue is a farmer and lives on the western side of the island. Her harvest is random: good if the wind is westerly, and bad if easterly. The probabilities of westerly and easterly are 50–50.

- If the wind is easterly, then Blue's harvest (in units of numeraire, or consumption) will only be 50.
- If it is westerly, it will be 100.

Blue is risk averse: *ex ante* (i.e., before the wind is known), she would rather have the certainty of consuming 75 instead of facing the uncertain prospect of consuming 50 with probability 0.5 and 100 with probability 0.5.

We can represent her *ex ante* preferences by indifference curves on a graph where the horizontal axis is labeled m_{BE} or "Blue's consumption if the wind is easterly" and the vertical axis is labeled m_{BW} or "Blue's consumption if the wind is westerly," see Figure 6.8. The 45° line is called the *certainty line*. Consumption is certain on the certainty line: points in there entail the same consumption whether the wind is easterly or westerly. We know that, because of risk aversion, she prefers point C, on the certainty line, to the initial endowment or "harvest" point ω_B, which has the same expected consumption as point C. Accordingly, the *ex ante* indifference curve going through C is higher than the one going through ω_B.

In general, risk aversion implies that the slope of the indifference curve at any point on the certainty line (if the indifference curve is smooth there) must be $-\pi/[1 - \pi]$. In Blue's example, $\pi = 1 - \pi = 0.5$, and the slope must be -1. This can be seen as follows. Suppose not: say, e.g., that her indifference curve is flatter than that, as illustrated by the curve through point $(75, 75)$ in Figure 6.9. Then point $(m_{BE}, m_{BW}) = (75 - \varepsilon, 75 + \varepsilon)$ for positive and small ε (say $(74, 76)$, as in the figure) would be preferred to $(75, 75)$, contradicting risk aversion, because $0.5 \times 74 + 0.5 \times 76 = 75$. By the same argument, the curve cannot be steeper than the straight

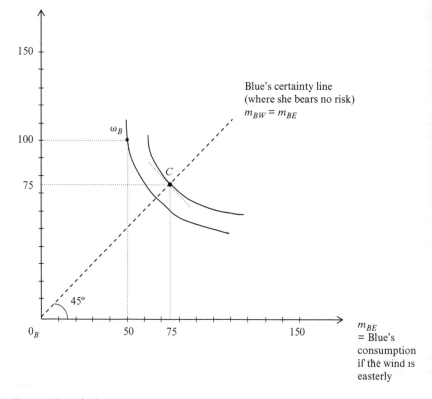

Figure 6.8   *Blue's* ex ante *preferences (risk averse)*

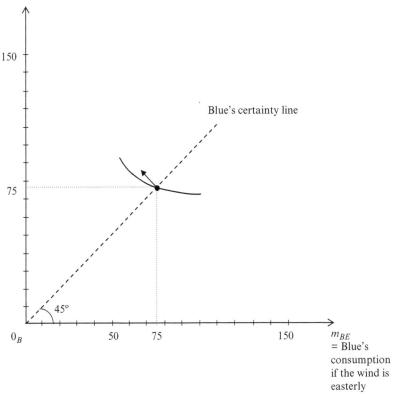

Figure 6.9   *The indifference curve must have the slope* $-\pi/[1 - \pi]$ *at any point on the certainty line*

line with slope -1. Hence, the slope of an indifference curve at its point of intersection with the certainty line must be -1. The proof generalizes to any probability π between zero and one, showing a slope of $-\pi/[1 - \pi]$ for any indifference curve at the point where it intersects the certainty line.

6.5   Efficient risk sharing

The notion of economic efficiency now requires the impossibility of making everybody *ex ante* better off, in which case we say that there is *ex ante* efficiency, which implies *efficient risk sharing* (or *efficient risk pooling*, or *efficient insurance*). This condition is similar to exchange efficiency under certainty, which requires the equality of the marginal rates of substitution of any two consumers (see Section 1.7.3 above), but relative to *ex ante* preferences.

Continuing with the island metaphor, assume that there is a second farmer, Mr. Red, on the east side of the island. The easterlies are good for him, in particular:

•   If the wind is easterly, then Red's harvest will be 100;
•   But if the wind is westerly, Red's harvest will only be 50.

Let Red be risk averse. Then his *ex ante* indifference curves will look as in Figure 6.10, where the horizontal axis is labeled m_{RE} or "Red's consumption if the wind is easterly" and the vertical axis is labeled m_{RW} or "Red's consumption if the wind is westerly." Again, his indifference curves have a slope of $-\pi/[1 - \pi] = -1$ at any point on his certainty line.

We organize the harvest data in Table 6.1, where we see that *there is no uncertainty in the aggregate harvest*: whether the wind blows from the east or from the west, the overall harvest (and consumption) in the island will be 150. In other words, there is individual risk, but no aggregate risk, in this economy. We construct an Edgeworth box in order to visualize *ex ante* efficient allocations: see Figure 6.11.[3]

---

[3] The Edgeworth box is constructed as follows. First, we rotate Mr. Red's graph 90° counterclockwise, so that his horizontal axis points left. Second, we flip it vertically, so that his vertical axis points down. Third, we superimpose it to Ms. Blue's in such a way that their endowment points coincide. The dimensions of the box are therefore the aggregate endowments. Each point in the box has four coordinates: two relative to Blue's axes, and two to the (inverted) Red's axes, and represents an *ex ante* feasible allocation of the total harvest. The condition of exchange efficiency, or equality of the marginal rates of substitution, is graphically equivalent, in the interior of the box, to the tangency between the indifference curves of the two consumers.

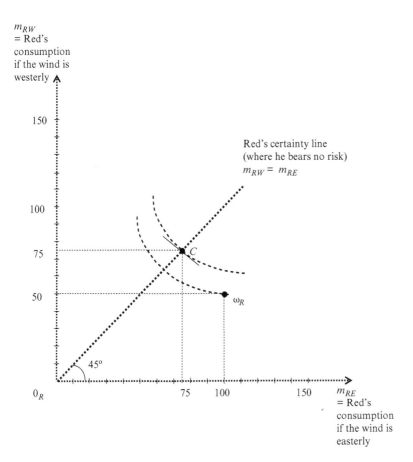

Figure 6.10   *Red's* ex ante *indifference curves (risk averse)*

Table 6.1 *No aggregate risk*

	State of nature	
	Easterly wind (prob. 0.5)	*Westerly wind (prob. 0.5)*
Harvests		
Ms. Blue	50	100
Mr. Red	100	50
Aggregate	150	150

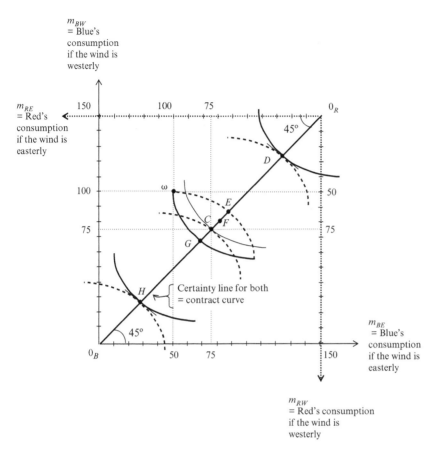

Figure 6.11   *The Edgeworth box in the absence of aggregate risk (both risk averse)*

Because of the absence of aggregate risk, the Edgeworth box is a square (150 by 150), and the certainty lines of Blue and Red coincide along its diagonal. At any such point along the diagonal, Blue's and Red's indifference curves have a slope of −1 and, therefore, they are tangent (their slopes differ anywhere outside the diagonal). This is precisely the equality of the marginal rates of substitution.[4] Thus, if both Blue and Red are risk averse, and there is no aggregate risk, then *ex ante efficiency* (or *efficient risk sharing) requires the elimination of all individual risks*, so that no person bears any risk or, in other words, all persons are fully insured. Graphically, the locus of efficient allocations, or *contract curve*, is the diagonal of the box, which coincides with the certainly lines of the two islanders. Any point on the diagonal, such as 0_B, *H, G, C, F, E, D*, or 0_R, *is ex ante* efficient.

The absence of aggregate risk is a special occurrence: there is aggregate risk in many realistic situations: for instance, aggregate profits and employment are procyclical in the business cycle. Let us modify the example in order to illustrate aggregate risk. Assume that (see Table 6.2):

- If the wind is easterly, then Blue's harvest will be 40;
- But if the wind is westerly, then Blue's harvest will be 100;

and:

- If the wind is easterly, then Red's harvest will be 80;
- But if the wind is westerly, then Red's the harvest will be 50.

Aggregate consumption is then higher (150) if the wind is westerly than if it is easterly (120). Thus, there is aggregate risk, implying that the Edgeworth box is not square: it is now a 120 by 150 rectangle. As in Figure 2.13, the two certainty lines are parallel and never meet. Thus it is impossible for both persons to be on their certainty lines: at least one person must bear some risk. In fact, both must bear some risk at any efficient allocation if both consumers are risk averse.

But if one of them is risk neutral, then he or she bears all risk. For instance, let Mr. Red be now risk neutral: he is indifferent among all points (m_{RE}, m_{RW}) with the same expected consumption $\pi\, m_{RE} + [1 - \pi]\, m_{RW}$, so that his indifference curves satisfy equations of the form $\pi\, m_{RE} + [1 - \pi]\, m_{RW} = Constant$, and are therefore straight lines of slope $-\pi/[1 - \pi]$, equal to −1 in our example, see Figure 6.12. Let Ms. Blue still be risk averse (as in Figure 6.8), so that her indifference curves have the slope $-\pi/[1 - \pi] = -1$ only at her certainty line. Then the Edgeworth box looks like Figure 6.13, and efficient risk sharing occurs at points such as C', where

---

[4] See Section 1.7 of Chapter 1 above.

Table 6.2 *Aggregate risk*

		State of nature	
		Easterly wind (prob. 0.5)	*Westerly wind (prob. 0.5)*
Harvests	Blue	40	100
	Red	80	50
	Aggregate	120	150

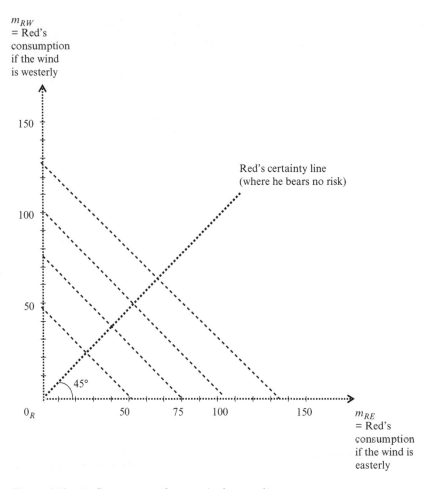

Figure 6.12   *Red's* ex ante *preferences (risk neutral)*

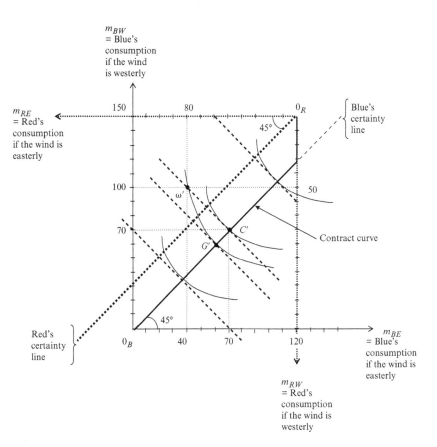

Figure 6.13   *The Edgeworth box in the presence of aggregate risk: Blue is risk averse and Red is risk neutral*

the indifference curves of Red and Blue are tangent: Blue is on her certainty line, and hence bears no risk, whereas risk-neutral Red bears all risk.

6.6   Risk-sharing entails *ex post* redistribution

Any point in the contract curve between E and G of Figure 6.11 also has the property of being preferred by both Blue and Red to their initial endowment (or harvest) points. Similarly, any point in the contract curve between points C' and G' of Figure 6.13 has the property of being preferred by Blue to the endowment point ω', and not worse for Red than the endowment point. (Red is indifferent between C' and the endowment point, but prefers any other point in that segment to the endowment point.) Thus, these points could in principle be the outcome of voluntary negotiations between Blue and Red, where all possible gains from negotiation are exhausted.[5] For instance, in the case of Table 6.1 and Figure 6.11, they can *ex ante* write an efficient risk-sharing contract by which, after (*ex post*) the wind is observed, the lucky person gives 25 units of the consumption good to the unlucky one, thus agreeing *ex ante* on point C in Figure 6.11. (For Table 6.2 and Figure 6.13, the *ex post* transfer is 30, reaching point C'.) It is in the nature of risk sharing arrangements that they are made *ex ante*, before the random event occurs, and that they result in an *ex post* transfer or redistribution from lucky to unlucky.

Instead of bilateral bargaining, we can think of Red being a large, risk neutral pool of insurance companies. In the case of Table 6.1 and Figure 6.11, we may interpret as a "loss" the 50 units of harvest that Blue does not get when the wind is easterly, relative to the westerly wind. The insurance market offers Blue the following contract. Before the wind is known, Blue pays a *premium* of 25. If the wind is westerly, then no further transaction happens, but if it is easterly, then the insurance companies pay Blue an *indemnity* (*compensation* or *settlement*) for her loss, of 50. Hence, no matter what the wind is, Blue consumes the certain amount of 75.

Many public expenditure programs, such as social security for old age and disability, unemployment insurance or health insurance through Medicare, provide social insurance, therefore reducing the risk borne by individuals. They all entail *ex post* redistribution from the lucky to the unlucky. For instance, an unemployment insurance program redistributes from the employed (the "lucky") to the unemployed (the "unlucky"). Considerations of both equity and efficiency are relevant for the analysis and design of such programs.

---

[5] See the discussion on bargaining in Section 3.6 of Chapter 3 above.

6.7   Actuarial fairness and *ex ante* redistribution

We say that an *ex ante* risk-sharing system, or insurance contract, is *actuarially fair* if, for every participant, the *expected net transfer is zero*. Consider point C in Figure 6.11. Blue will receive 25 units with probability 0.5 (if the wind is easterly) and give up 25 units also with probability 0.5. The *actuarial value* or *expected net transfer* of this scheme for her is $0.5 \times 25 + 0.5 \times [-25] = 0$. Similarly, the actuarial value of this scheme for Red is also zero; accordingly, such a scheme is actuarially fair, where the word "fair" is used in a purely algebraic sense, devoid of normative meaning.

More generally, consider an scheme under which a consumer receives z_1 units of numeraire with probability π and pays z_2 with probability $1 - \pi$. Then for her, the scheme is

- *actuarially fair* if $\pi z_1 - [1 - \pi] z_2 = 0 \left(or \; \dfrac{z_2}{z_1} = \dfrac{\pi}{1 - \pi} \right)$,

- *actuarially favorable* if $\pi z_1 - [1 - \pi] z_2 > 0 \left(or \; \dfrac{z_2}{z_1} < \dfrac{\pi}{1 - \pi} \right)$,

- *actuarially unfavorable* if $\pi z_1 - [1 - \pi] z_2 < 0 \left(or \; \dfrac{z_2}{z_1} > \dfrac{\pi}{1 - \pi} \right)$.

Actuarial fairness is synonymous with the absence of *ex ante* redistribution. Of course, as argued in Section 6.6 above, implementing an actuarially fair scheme does require an *ex post* redistribution.

But consider point F of Figure 6.11, with coordinates (80, 80), for Blue and (70, 70) for Red, an efficient allocation where, *ex ante*, both are better off than at their initial endowment points (F lies between E and G). Point F is actuarially favorable to Blue, because if the winds are easterly she receives 30, whereas if the winds are westerly she gives up 20. Thus, the actuarial value of this scheme for Blue is $0.5 \times 30 + 0.5 \times [-20] = 5$. Similarly, the actuarial value of the scheme for Red is -5. There is *ex ante* redistribution in Blue's favor.

Perhaps Point F could result from an efficient negotiation between Blue and Red where Blue has superior bargaining skills. (See the discussion of bargaining in Section 3.6 above.) Or perhaps, because of her metabolism, Blue must consume higher amounts than Red in order to achieve the same level of welfare, and public policy compensates for her handicap. In any event, normative analysis cannot be solely based on the presence or absence of actuarial redistribution.

6.8 Asymmetrical information in insurance

We have seen that, in the market for lemons, asymmetrical information could preclude economic efficiency. This also occurs in insurance markets, which suffer from two effects of asymmetrical information, namely *moral hazard* and *adverse selection*.

The problem of moral hazard lies on the dependence of behavior on insurance: being insured may increase the probability or magnitude of a loss, because it then becomes rational to be less careful in prevention (if your house is insured against fire, an expensive fire alarm system becomes less attractive). This problem can be alleviated with deductibles or coinsurance, which require the insured to bear some risk.

The market for lemons has evidenced the effect of adverse selection: lemons drive peaches out of the market. In insurance, consumers aware of being high risk will have a strong incentive to buy insurance. If information is asymmetrical, so that the insurer has poorer information about individual risks than the buyer of insurance, high risk individuals ("lemons") may drive low risks ("peaches") out of the insurance market, creating *ex ante* inefficiency.

We can apply to insurance the three cases analysed in the market for lemons of Section 6.3 above. Let ρ denote the fraction of high-risk consumers in society. Assume for simplicity that the effects of an illness can be reduced to a loss of J units of numeraire for either type: the wealth of Consumer i is ω_i if healthy, and $\omega_i - J$ if ill. The probability of illness is π^H for a high-risk consumer, and π^L for a low-risk one, with $\pi^H > \pi^L$.

Assume that, because of competition among insurance companies, the expected profit of each company is zero. Suppose that the consumer can buy one of two levels of insurance: *full insurance*, with indemnity for illness equal to J, so that the insured does not bear any risk, and *minimal insurance*, where the indemnity is only $J^M < J$. In either case, when insured, Consumer i's *ex post* consumption if healthy is $\omega_i - Premium$, and, if ill, $\omega_i - Premium - Loss + Indemnity$.

Case 1: Information is symmetrical and good
As in the lemons example, we have two separate markets. Both groups choose full insurance, high-risk (resp. low-risk) consumers paying the fair premium $\pi^H J$ (resp. $\pi^L J$), and an *ex ante* efficient allocation is reached.

Case 2: Information is symmetrical and bad
If information is symmetrical and bad, then neither consumers nor insurance companies can tell high- from low-risk consumers. Accordingly, both buyers and sellers of insurance take the average probability

$\bar{\pi} := \rho\pi^H + [1 - \rho]\pi^L$ as the probability of illness. All consumers choose full insurance at the premium $\bar{\pi}J$, reaching an *ex ante* efficient allocation.

Case 3: Asymmetrical information
Any consumer can now tell whether she is high or low risk, but insurance companies cannot. Accordingly, the insurance market has to offer the same contracts to all consumers. As in the lemons example, the high risks may drive the low risks out of the market. Even if low-risk consumers are risk averse, they may decide not to fully insure at the average premium $\bar{\pi}J$, and, *a fortiori*, at any higher premium. In that case, the market equilibrium is inefficient, because only high-risk consumers choose full insurance.

6.9   Minimal guaranteed insurance

Even in countries without compulsory health insurance, hospital emergency rooms cannot turn away uninsured patients. This can be interpreted as the public provision, taxpayer financed, of a minimal level of health insurance at zero premium. It could create a "market failure" if some risk-averse agents prefer the minimal free level of insurance to full insurance at a market premium. As long as insurance companies are risk neutral, the outcome is then *ex ante* inefficient because some risk-averse consumers are not fully insured. This inefficiency may be targeted by compulsory insurance, to which we turn.

6.10   Compulsory insurance

When the market equilibrium is inefficient because of adverse selection or minimal guaranteed insurance, efficiency can be reached by compulsory full insurance. But, as seen in the discussion of the market for lemons, whether compulsion Pareto dominates, in the *ex ante* sense, the market equilibrium depends on parameter values. If it does not, then compulsory insurance entails *ex ante* redistribution.

For instance, in the adverse selection model of Section 6.8 above, compulsory full insurance at the average premium $\bar{\pi}J$ may Pareto dominate the market equilibrium. But for some parameter values low-risk consumers may be worse off than at the market equilibrium, in which case compulsory insurance implies an *ex ante* redistribution favoring high risks. (Of course, high-risk consumers are better off under compulsory insurance, because they get full insurance at a lower premium.) Similarly, the minimal level of insurance discussed in 6.9 entails *ex ante* redistribution from taxpayers to those who take the free minimal insurance: this particular form of *ex ante* redistribution may be replaced, under the compulsory insurance policy, by other types of *ex ante* redistribution.

Are such redistributions just? To the extent that risks are independent from the decisions, past and present, of the individual (say, they are due to sex, age or genes), then the ethical principle of equality of opportunity favors compulsory insurance. But this is not the case if risk is due to conditions which are under the control of the individual (such as smoking). These are issues of distributive justice, distinct from efficiency.

The previous argument for compulsory insurance has also been applied to income risks, including unemployment risks, and catastrophic risks. Anti-poverty programs, in particular those targeting child poverty, can be understood as compulsory insurance against the lottery of life. Again, compulsory insurance is *ex ante* efficient, but may or may not Pareto dominate the market outcome.

There is a general nexus between *ex ante* insurance and *ex post* redistribution, because the aim of any insurance system is to reduce the *ex post* inequality between the lucky and the unlucky. We conclude with the words of Jacques Drèze:[6]

> the existence of risk-sharing arrangements reduces the urge for corrective redistribution; conversely, their absence reinforces that urge. Many public policies, like progressive taxation or unemployment insurance, are a mixture of indemnities reflecting ex ante efficient insurance schemes on the one hand and ex post redistributive transfers on the other. The mixture of the two components is seldom identified explicitly, and there is an inescapable element of ambiguity in the meaning of ex ante. Thus, redistribution of income from high-skilled to low-skilled wage earners could be viewed as risk-sharing among unborn individuals uncertain about their native skills.

---

[6] J.H. Drèze (1993), "Can varying social insurance contributions improve labour market efficiency?" in Anthony B. Atkinson, editor, *Alternatives to Capitalism: The Economics of Partnership*, New York: St. Martin Press, p. 166.

Index